WIFE

To: Daniellie,

Continue to be wisely Inspired

Faithfully Empowered!

Many blessings,

Praise for

WIFE

"I love Dr. Eddie's book trilogy *Dear Queen, Woman,* and now *WIFE.*
The previous books gave us valuable tools on how to overcome
brokenness, bitterness, unhappy relationships, and know our worth.
To complete this process, Dr. Eddie Connor has given us another
outstanding book, *WIFE* 'Wisely Inspired Faithfully Empowered.'
I love how he references that the word "wife" is more than a title. It's
actually a function. Oftentimes, we are more focused on the title and
the ring. However, it doesn't mean a thing if you are with the wrong
person. This book has helped me to realize the true purpose of
marriage and maintain a meaningful, long-lasting relationship with
my future husband. This is an amazing book that everyone must read!"

- Dr. LaTonya S. Cross, *DNP*

"In a time where much emphasis is placed on finding 'the one,' this
book will encourage the reader to prioritize on becoming 'the one.'
What a novel concept that every single person should hear! Dr. Eddie
Connor brings a very healthy, practical Christian perspective to
singleness that the church and the world needs to hear. Hear ye him!"

- Pastor Kellen Brooks, *Pentecostal Temple COGIC*

"Dr. Eddie Connor has written a go-to guide for single men and
women who desire to be married! *WIFE* is a must-read primer to
prepare and find your purpose partner. This well-articulated piece,
offers sharp and penetrating insights into seemingly complex issues.
I applaud Dr. Eddie's unparalleled forthrightness, God-given
conviction, and ability to articulate a message that is desperately
needed!"

- Timipre Wolo, *Esq.*

"*WIFE*, 'Wisely Inspired Faithfully Empowered': what an empowering and uplifting acronym for the treasure that God designed a woman to be. Dr. Eddie Connor succinctly and strategically speaks into the lives of those preparing for marriage. This book may be entitled, *WIFE*; but, it will inspire the man or woman in our life. Proverbs 18:22 (KJV) reminds us, "Whoso findeth a wife findeth a good thing, and obtaineth favor of the Lord." Dr. Connor reminds us that a woman is already a wife when she is found by her husband. And, he encourages a woman who desires to be a wife to prepare so that when she is found, she will have become what she desires. In addition, Dr. Connor brings a transparency that allows us to see glimpses of lessons that he has learned. He candidly speaks from a male perspective, to encourage men to be ready to be husbands by already possessing purpose, place, presence, and power. Upon reading this book, you will not want to put it down. And, you will want to sow it into the lives of others so that their lives will be blessed by the wealth of knowledge and insight pouring from its pages. Get your book clubs, sister circle and man power groups together because you will want to dialogue and discuss the numerous nuggets in the book, *WIFE*."

- **Dr. Tiffany Stinson**, Pharm.D., *Pharmacist/Evangelist/Speaker*

"As a woman prepares for her wedding day, she reminisces of fairy tales told as a child. Girls often dream of prince charming one day coming to their rescue. The idealization of happily ever after, puts up a façade on the true meaning of marriage. In this book, Dr. Eddie Connor takes us on a journey through holy matrimony. He presents a master plan for women prepared to become the *WIFE,* that a man prayed and asked God to grant. As you read, begin to think about the royal transitions from *Dear Queen* to *Woman* and now *WIFE!*"

- **Ivy Nichole Neal**, Founder of *Let's Have Girl Talk Mentoring*

"We live in a microwave society, laden with a gallimaufry of emotions and opinions. Dr. Eddie Connor enriches us with a timely, real, raw and relevant masterpiece! At the core of humans is ingrained the need for love and acceptance. Yet navigating the murky waters of emotional turbulence and the sense of a lack of purpose has birthed apathy. *WIFE* is an engaging, impact-loaded flow of wisdom that will reignite your passion for purpose, renew your thinking, and strategically equip you for new levels in life and relationships. Men and women will grow from pain to purpose and change the narrative, waltzing harmoniously as 'Wisely Inspired Faithfully Empowered' purpose partners!"

- **Dr. Maureen Benjamin**, *Pharm.D.*

"Dr. Eddie Connor's book *WIFE* is an amazing creative instrument for all readers! His reflection reveals a practical phenomenon – all men aren't husbands and all women aren't wives! Whether married, divorced or single, this book is sure to break generational curses, dismiss all myths, and ultimately free the minds of every reader – by educating them with a Biblical and practical study of a *WIFE*! I foresee this as a guide, for sharing the precious secrets that reveal the true Godly character of a ready bride! The angle of a woman is right and the view of a man is rare! Truly, Dr. Eddie Connor is considered a 'permanent marker' to a fast eroding society!"

- **Minister Ryan D. Rutley**, *Psalms Group Studios, C.E.O.*

"Are you ready to be someone's husband or wife? Do you know how to function as a husband or wife? The book *WIFE* by Dr. Eddie Connor is a blueprint, on how to prepare as a husband or wife in your singleness. This book will restore your faith in knowing that God will prepare you for the relationship of a lifetime, while preparing your spouse for you."

- **Rachel G. Woodson**, *Relationship Expert*

ALSO BY DR. EDDIE CONNOR

Purposefully Prepared to Persevere

Collections of Reflections,
Volumes 1-3: Symphonies of Strength

E.CON the ICON: from Pop Culture to
President Barack Obama

Unwrap The Gift In You

Heal Your Heart

My Brother's Keeper

Dear Queen

WIFE

Becoming the Right One
for the Right One

DR. EDDIE CONNOR

norbrook
publishing

Also available as an eBook and Audiobook from Norbrook Publishing.

Library of Congress Cataloging-in-Publication Data is available upon
request.

ISBN 978-0-9970504-8-6
eBook ISBN 978-0-9970504-9-3

PRINTED IN THE UNITED STATES OF AMERICA

10 9 8 7 6 5 4 3 2 1

First Edition

May you become what you desire to receive,
as a purpose partner, husband, and wife for life.

*"He who finds a **WIFE** finds a good thing and obtains favor from the Lord."*
- Proverbs 18:22 -

CONTENTS

WIFE

INTRODUCTION

There are two questions that people often ask me. The first is "How old are you?" In which I reply, "I'm older than Michael B. Jordan and younger than Michael Jordan." I think that answer gives people a good reference, from what spectrum of years to categorize me in. The second and most unyielding question is, "When are you going to get married?" People ask me as if I'm unemployed and can't find a job. It's a rather intrusive, interrogating, finger-pointing, and under the microscope type of questioning. Why rush me into, what should last for a lifetime?

I pause to ponder about my last two bestselling books. They said I wasn't supposed to write *Dear Queen* because I didn't have one. They said I couldn't write *Woman* because

I'm not one. Some will now say, "How can he write *Wife* when he doesn't have one?" We are so inundated with possession that we rarely process the power of perception. People have been telling me what I can't do all of my life. When I had cancer they told me I can't make it. They told me I couldn't go to college. They said I can't thrive in my career.

None of it stopped me. It only propelled me. Skeptics and critics won't stop me, from preparing to be a great husband to my future wife for life. All of it fuels me and just adds another chapter to my life's journey. So, as they're talking I keep writing, just as you're reading. Dear sir or ma'am everything I'm not, made me everything I am. I've come to the realization that people who judge books by their covers, generally do so because they can't read. People should read your story, before they judge your journey.

As you delve into this didactic treatise, you will see that the content will illuminate your character. Much of today's relationship content, often promotes women becoming wives but not men becoming husbands. Maybe I was also a contributor, to that school of thought via previous books. However, I want to provide balance with this one.

From the time girls are born, they are groomed to be strong women and wives. On the contrary, are men prepared to be equally strong husbands? Who is teaching and training boys and men to be good husbands? We do a great job of making women good wives. How do we make men better husbands? If you were raised like me without a good father and husband example, then you often ask yourself the question "Can I be a good husband, if I never saw my father be a good one to my mother?" These are thought provoking questions, that many people don't take the time to address and assess.

I've heard time and time again, "You will be what you see." How can our boys and men become good husbands and fathers, if they didn't see one? How do you play a role, if you weren't given a script? Is it easier for a woman to become a wife, more than a man to become a husband? Oftentimes, society promulgates the virtues and values of a woman, by making it a double standard, to do what men have done or even continue to do. The standards and virtues we extol upon women are rarely achieved by mere mortal men.

The book *Wife* is for single men who desire to be married and for single women, who desire to marry a good man. I've written books for men. I've written books for women. Now this book is written for both men and women. Somewhere deep interpersonally within me, I'm writing about what I desire…a wife. Sometimes you have to write about what you're desiring, until you get what you're expecting. In other words if I write about it, I just might attract it.

You may say or think, what business does a single man have writing a book called *Wife*? Yes, it's the elephant in the reading room. However, you can have the title or position but not be able to function. You don't have to be a wife, to tell a woman what she should look for in a man. Much less how a man should prepare and improve his life to find a wife. You can have the qualifications, but if you're not a quality person what does it mean?

This book offers a powerful perspective on how to prepare, for what God has prepared for you to receive. Beyond the scrutiny and insecurity, I want to speak to your real identity. There must be a compass and standard of what to look for, what to become, and how to overcome.

Undoubtedly, social media has led to relationship apathy for dating, courting, and marrying. As a result, many people are settling, just so they can say they have somebody. What is it to connect with someone, but be disconnected from God and yourself? It makes no sense to know them, but

5

not know Him. What is it for you to know who they are, but not know who you are? There must be a place in your life, where you have fulfillment and joy that does not come at the expense of someone else.

People can make you happy, but only God can give you joy. Happiness is based on what's happening, but joy is ever-flowing despite the situation you're experiencing. When it comes to relationships, a lot of people are rushing. However, are we becoming what we intend on receiving? Some people want what they can't have. They have what they can't keep and end up keeping what they don't want.

According to the American Psychological Association, "50% of marriages end in divorce and the divorce rate among those who remarry is even higher." Nothing seems to last and what lasts doesn't satisfy. So many times we are focused on the physical and superficial, but not the true foundation of what is spiritual. Our society is obsessed with the carat size of a ring, but not the size of one's character.

Maybe you even analyzed the ring, on the cover of this book. A purpose partner, husband, or wife is more focused on the foundation of character than carats. A fancy wedding, seems to be more important than a faithful marriage these days.

Many men want a wife, but are they ready for one? Many women want the title of wife, but do they act like one? You don't just become a husband or wife, when you get a ring and wed in holy matrimony. You become one through the process of preparation. There are some men and women who have been married for years, but they're still not husband and wife. They are just roommates with the title of spouse. It's a loveless marriage, in a house that's not a home.

Sometimes you're a husband in training to a future wife that's waiting. When you find her, she will already be what you desire. More than the title of wife, she possesses the qualities to be a great wife and improve your life. You're a wife when he finds you, but you're his wife when he marries you.

Keep in mind, we are living in times where the institution of marriage is under attack. People will commit to the terms of a phone contract, before they do to each other. Love seems to be just a tattoo. Loyalty is only a song on the radio. Baby showers are more frequent than weddings. Being a "wifey" is more popular than becoming a wife. To be called someone's "bae" seems to be more important than becoming a husband these days. To be "boo'd up" seems to be more significant than a marriage covenant.

Undoubtedly, I'm influenced by great leaders and orators, but even more I'm inspired by great songwriters. Yes, the mellifluous music and euphonious melody, but more importantly their lyrical vulnerability. To be able to wear your heart on your sleeve, unmask your emotions, communicate compassionately, and express yourself is true freedom. This is a book where I'm placing myself under the microscope, in order to express what is oftentimes repressed.

As we aspire higher, the lights don't only show our strengths but also our struggles. It shows our glory and our story. Our triumphs but also our trials. The book *Wife* is one of truth and transparency, unfurled to bring unity to our personal identity. Ultimately, it prepares us for greater love and opportunities.

I'm literally taking my own medicine. As I write to you, I'm talking to myself too. I realize that it's rare to do that in a society that champions hypermasculinity, rather than one's vulnerability. Oftentimes, each day is like Halloween because we go through life wearing a mask. We even adopt a Superman or Superwoman syndrome, but the costume becomes our kryptonite.

The "S" on our chest doesn't always mean we're strong. Sometimes it symbolizes that we're sad, sensitive, and struggling. In this case it means we're single, but it should also mean that we're selective. Just because you can have anybody, doesn't mean you should settle for just anybody. God wants you to have the right somebody. Your time of singleness should be a place of preparedness, maturation, purposeful living, and wholeness.

Until you press past your past and get over an ex, don't go looking for your next. Relationships are not bandaids and void fillers. How can you heal what you continue to conceal? How can you address what you won't confess? You can't recover from what you've covered, until you take the time to uncover it.

Yes, it's true that no one can wear their crown like a *Dear Queen*. No one can get your attention like a *Woman*. However, no one can improve your life, like a wonderful *Wife*. I define the word **WIFE** as *Wisely Inspired Faithfully Empowered*. Who God has created her to be and the power of knowing her identity, can't be replaced. Through tough times, rejection, isolation, and failed connections, she will still become what she was created to be. As a man in pursuit of a wife, we must know that the favor on her life increases our ability to provide for our wife. Her virtue is priceless. Her wisdom is matchless. Her words of inspiration will propel you into greater success. She's empowered to do more, even with less. This kind of woman is a benefit and a necessity.

As you read *Wife*, begin to envision yourself as a purpose partner who God is preparing, to be a blessing to someone's life. You will never seize what you fail to see. The intangible traits, gifts, untapped potential, and vision that you possess within is enough for the right one. You don't have to reduce yourself, to fit in with someone who is intimidated by you. Whoever is intimidated will soon be eliminated.

Remove limited thinking from your mentality due to the past, missteps, hurts, and mistakes. You are the right type, so prepare for your prototype. As you're waiting keep working, growing, and developing for the person you intend on receiving. It will happen for you, in the process of working the vision that God gave you. For all of the times you've asked, "When will it be my time?" Know that what's for you won't pass you. It's tailor-made and it will align at the right time. In the end it's better to wait long, than to marry wrong. When you know that you will receive the best, you can rejoice and find happiness in your singleness. You can prepare to be a husband to your future wife. You can celebrate as a future wife, knowing that you will enhance your husband's life.

Reach out and let me know, how this book has inspired you. I often say, "The revolution will not be televised. It will be digitized."

Please connect with me at **EddieConnor.com** for more information and inspiration. Friend and follow me via Facebook, Instagram, and Twitter: **@EddieConnorJr**. Take a photo with your book. Post it on your social media sites and include the hashtag *#WifeTheBook*.

Are you ready for marriage or just a wedding? To

have the title of husband and wife or actually do the work to become one? I'm excited to embark on this journey with you, as we prepare for our purpose partner. Speak life over your life. You will be a great husband and *WIFE!*

CHAPTER 1

Singleness Means Wholeness

When you walk in healing and wholeness, you will attract people who live in their greatness not brokenness.

Y ou can be alone and not lonely. A lot of times we look for people and things, to fill the voids in our lives. Sometimes we run back, to the same people who crippled us and caused us to cry. We return looking for those who kidnapped us emotionally, to rescue us entirely. The past isn't offering anything new. Don't look back. You can't expect the people who hurt you, to heal the wounds they caused you.

Realize that you will always feel empty, when you rely on people to pour into you. As a result, feeling lonely and incomplete will be the lot of your life. God is your source, not people. Stop looking for someone to complete you. Only God does that. They cannot do for you naturally, what God can do for you spiritually. You will never make forward progress, by holding on to that which causes you to regress. You were created to leap into your future, not limp through life by living in your past. Walk by faith into wholeness.

TAKE THAT TO THE BANK

I don't know about you, but I love long romantic walks to the bank. Maybe you like long romantic walks on the beach, but I prefer the bank. When you go to the bank, you can only withdraw according to the amount of money that is in your account. If you use more than what is allotted to you, an overdraft occurs. This particular deficit is based on withdrawing more money than the account holds. How many times have people made more withdrawals, than deposits in your life? Too often, we have allowed people access into the bank account of our lives. They were not accountable and discounted your value. They withdrew from your peace, love, hope, energy, ideas, loyalty, respect, and resources. As a result, they ultimately withdrew themselves when they got what they desired. You have been through enough that would have depleted you. Allow God to complete His purpose through you. Realize that you are the CEO: Chief Encouraging Officer of your life. You have the ability to hire and fire. Don't allow people to break you and bankrupt you.

ASSETS VERSUS LIABILITIES

We have allowed people to make more withdrawals than deposits in our lives, which ultimately leaves us broken and bankrupt. You have had enough liabilities. When will you surround yourself with assets? Liabilities lead to a loss of identity, purpose, time, ideas, investments, and dreams. Assets add and strengthen you. They cause you to gain in the places you would have lost. Assets cause your value to appreciate, liabilities cause you to depreciate. Do you know your value? When you recognize that God placed a treasure within, then despite what you face you are never without. He will sustain you in times of doubt, distress, and what seemingly depletes the essence of you. Be careful of who you allow into your space. Every relationship is a power encounter. It will either add to or subtract from your value. Make sure the people in your life don't bankrupt you, but empower you to breakthrough.

ONE IS A WHOLE NUMBER

I've truly had some great achievements in my life, by matriculating through the collegiate ranks in higher levels of academia. However, still to this day I'm more English than Math. My expertise is more versed in words than in numbers. I can recall learning about whole numbers in middle school. My teacher informed me and my classmates, that the number one is a whole number. In essence, the number one is not attached to fractions, decimals, or negative numbers. Sometimes math equations have life applications. As one person with one life to live, why should you allow people and what you've been through to reduce you? As a single person, you must not live from a place of brokenness but wholeness.

Do the math in your own life. If people aren't adding to your life, then do some simple math and subtract them from your life. Stop allowing what you've been through to fracture you, decimate you, and make you feel negative about who God made you. Don't attach yourself to those who disrespect, disappoint, and diminish the value in you. God will give you double for your trouble and turn your tragedy to strategy. God will add to and multiply your life. He will turn your brokenness into wholeness. Only God can fill the void and hole, when you allow Him to make you whole.

WILL YOU BE MADE WHOLE?

John 5:5-9 tells the story of how Jesus healed a man, who had an infirmity for 38 years. It seems as if Jesus asked an unintelligent, if not a sarcastic question to the man. Jesus said "Wilt thou be made whole?" I mean Jesus, don't you see the man's condition? Why would you ask him this question, as you can clearly see the state of his situation? Don't you think he wants to be healed and whole? It's interesting that the scripture never shared the man's name, just the nature of his circumstance. He was classified as an impotent man. The state of his situation, superseded the name that he was given. We don't know his name. All we know is his situation.

So many times as men, we are categorized by what we do and what we have experienced but not by the essence of who we are. Some of our brothers are known by their mistakes. They're known for being in the streets, fatherless, incarcerated, or as hustlers. We are known by our weaknesses but not our strengths. As a result, we lay in the pain of our situation but not the power of our revelation. Jesus asked the man did he want to be made whole, because his situation communicated the fact that he didn't want to be. Nothing about the man, affirmed that he wanted to be made well. The impotent man pointed his finger and blamed everyone around him, for the state of his own condition. He declared, "I have no one to put me in the pool. As I am coming, someone steps in before me." How many excuses have you made? How many times have you played the blame game or watched other people do the same?

MISERY LOVES COMPANY

Keep in mind, he is laying in the company of people who are just like him. The people around him are impotent, void of power, blind, and withered. How long will you lay around and stay around people, who live their life helpless and

powerless? You can't expect more, if you settle for less.
Why hang around people who have no vision and are
withered by worry? The people you surround yourself with,
are a direct reflection of who you are and how you think.

We always say, "Hurt people, hurt people." We must
also know that hurting people, hang around hurting people.
Misery loves company. Light doesn't hang out with
darkness. If you keep hanging around people who are
negative, despondent, and mean spirited then you will
eventually belike them too. Just like you are what you eat.
You are who you hang around. Your association brings about
assimilation. The people who you surround yourself with,
will either preserve you or consume you. They will bless you
or stress you. Get around people who are leaping, not
limping.

How many times have you made excuses, for why
you are where you are? You've pointed the blame at other

people for your brokenness. You say, "If this didn't happen to me I would have been here. If so and so didn't do this and if such and such didn't hurt me like that, I would be in a better place." Stop laying on your bed of brokenness, misery, and affliction. Rise to walk with determination.

EXCUSES FOR CIRCUMSTANCES

In this scripture, it's as if Jesus interrupted the man's excuses. He said, "Rise, pick up your bed and walk." Immediately the man was whole. Now why wouldn't Jesus tell the man to leave his bed? Simply because the man's embarrassment now became his testimony. The bed I was laying on, I'm now carrying home. The bed represents the scar. Him being made whole took away the pain. How many times have we been like the impotent man, making excuses for our circumstances? Excuses for why you haven't written the book or started the business. Excuses because you're divorced. Excuses because you've been hurt, neglected, and rejected.

For years, I laid on my bed of affliction from the diagnosis of cancer, feeling sorry for myself. I laid on the excuses of people's rejection and my father's lack of protection. I laid on my lazy bed of doubt, depression, and thoughts of suicide. I reclined in remorse. I stretched out on my struggles. I laid on my bed of brokenness and insecurity. I suppose that I could have lived, by lying in repose. However, I decided to shake off sadness, struggles, and setbacks. I had to make up my mind that I wanted to be made whole. The Lord healed me and now I have the victory over what was hindering me.

How bad do you want your healing? Do you really want to be made whole? You've prayed and cried over it. You've been angry about it. You've blamed everybody because of it. What will you do to get a breakthrough from it? God is calling you to rise above it. He will bring testimonies out of your brokenness, to bless someone else.

HURTS TO BE HAPPY

God will not disturb you, if you like the condition you're in. The impotent man was surviving, but not thriving in a place of healing. God will not force you to be free. So many people sabotage their own success because of their insecurity. They don't feel that they are lovable or valuable. So, when they connect to someone who will love them, they run away. They focus on all of the wrong things. For them nothing is right unless something is wrong. As a result, we have learned how to function in dysfunction.

Some people are so broken by the pain of their past, to where it hurts to be happy. Yes, I'm talking about them, but I want you to think about you. What self-sabotaging behaviors are you engaged in that keeps you broken, wounded, withered, blind, and impotent?

A lot of times we abandon a good thing because it's foreign to us. We know what to expect from toxicity and even though it hurts us, we find shelter in what shackles us. The enemy will keep you oppressed and at the same time, make you fall in love with your oppressor.

HOW BAD DO YOU WANT IT?

How bad do you want to be healed? How bad do you want to be made whole? How bad do you want to move from where you are, to where you were created to be? You know how to survive, but now it's your time to thrive! All that you've been through, God has not forgotten you.

So often we find contentment in our calamity. We get so used to pain until we become numb to it. So many people are hobbling hopelessly through life and they're comfortable with it, just like the impotent man was for 38 years. Every year it's the same thing because you do the same thing. You're still limping but not leaping. You're still laying out but not rising up.

Have you ever been so sad, to where you forgot what

joy felt like? Have you ever been so sick, to where you forgot what being well feels like? Sometimes we've been stuck in our situation for so many years, that we have now settled and affirmed this is how things will always be. If you want the best, then you've got to rise from your bed of brokenness. Rise from the comfort of your calamity and chaos. Rise from your bed of abandonment. You have to make up in your mind to say, "Enough is enough." Rise from your bed of affliction and excuses, to go after it. Go after your joy. Go after your peace. Go after your blessing. Go after your healing!

ADDICTED TO BEING AFFLICTED

The one person that you've been looking to change your life, is the one standing in the mirror looking back at you. It's reflecting back at what you're reading. Sometimes we're addicted to the pain of what keeps us afflicted. Despite how bad the relationships have been and how hurt we have become, we still reflect on the good times. We are so nostalgic that even the emotional pain, becomes a place of mental and physical pleasure.

So many times we've become addicted to the pain of what's known, that we fail to leave it for the blessing that is foreign and unknown. When you've been in situations of depression, dismay, and doubt you become cynical. You literally live your life in cyclical circumstances. When you're not healed, you become skeptically suspicious of people and look for the bad in those who are good to you. Even when you step into avenues of peace, you look for chaos because you live from a place of brokenness and not wholeness.

I CHALLENGE YOU

What does not challenge you, will not change you. In this social media age there are plenty of dancing and singing challenges, but will you take the challenge to develop your greatness? Will you challenge yourself to aspire higher? Will

you challenge yourself to take off the mask? Will you

challenge yourself to heal from the vestiges of your past?

Will you accept the challenge to rise to the occasion? Will

you take the challenge to embrace the real you and love

yourself, despite the ugly situations you've been through?

When you commit to that challenge, you will see sustainable

change.

DELIVERED BUT NOT HEALED

It's true that you can be delivered but not healed. You're no

longer in the situation that brought the pain, but your mind

and heart are still battling and enraptured with the pain. You

can be out of a situation physically, but still be trapped and

connected to the hurt mentally. Too many people are

psychologically incarcerated, because of the brokenness they

have not healed from internally.

The aspects of wholeness may very well need to

encompass more than just prayer. We must include prayer with counseling, therapy, and self-care. It should not be regarded as something that is taboo. It's needed for me and you. Mental health is our wealth. All of the money, clothes, or makeup in the world can't cover a sad soul. Don't allow a stigma to make you a statistic. What you went through doesn't define you, it only refines you. We say, "Take your burdens to the Lord and leave them there." However, we also need to pick up wisdom, joy, peace, guidance, and a supportive system. It will help us get from there, to where we need to be. Healing is not always episodic. Sometimes it's a process that you have to continually address.

So often as men, we are screaming silently. We have been socialized to keep the pain inside. We have been raised to categorize pain as weakness leaving the body. As a result, many times we are afraid to open up to anyone, for the sake of appearing and being labeled as "soft and weak." Due to these factors we don't verbalize, we internalize. We have dangerously feminized being vulnerable, as if it's only something that girls and women are allowed to be. We know how to be open sexually but we're closed socially, emotionally, communicatively, and spiritually. We hide behind "mythical masculinity" which is a veneer for the toxicity we haven't healed from. We know how to be tough, but do we know how to love? We know how to compete, but can we collaborate to complete God's purpose for our lives?

Heaven forbid sister, you find yourself dating or in a relationship with a man who doesn't know how to communicate. He may even have no desire to. These days what is communication anymore? Do people still talk or do they just text? So, if you communicate and he doesn't, you may say to him "Why don't you open up?" Maybe that man has not been taught how to. Yes, he knows how to touch and what to say to you, to try and get what he wants from you. However, he doesn't know how to communicate with you.

God forbid brother, you find yourself in a relationship

with a woman who you are communicating with and she betrays your openness. When issues arise and disagreements ensue, she uses your experiences against you. As a result, you now close the emotional vault door of your life. It was initially hard to open and now you promise yourself to never release it again.

SAVAGE

The tale of two examples often makes us jaded, hurt, and broken when it comes to relationships. Many times our situations and skewed societal standards, have made us into emotional savages. If we don't watch it, our brokenness will make us barbaric. However, being a savage still won't heal that hole in your heart. Hurting someone else won't heal you. Being a savage will keep you living below average and beneath your privilege. You know what it's like to hurt and be hurt, but do you know what it's like to heal? Healing is not an overnight instance, it's a continual process. When you begin to trust God and experience His love, there will be healing that flows through your life. God will show you how to love yourself and as a result, love others.

This is why the Bible declares, "Be renewed in the spirit of your mind" (Ephesians 4:23). Based on what you're thinking dictates where you're going. Until you're healed, the spouse, purpose partner, destiny, and opportunity, will not truly be revealed in your life. God will delay it because He doesn't want you to damage it. Could it be that the person standing between you and the fulfillment of your spouse is you? I know it may not be what you want to read. This book is not written to tell you what you want to hear, but it's for what you need to hear. I'd rather give you the bitter truth over a sweet lie.

How can you be prepared, if you're only given words of celebration but it lacks instruction? Could it be that you're standing in your own way? I've started to pray a simple prayer and that is "God heal me, so you can reveal who is for me." The healing brings a greater level of discerning. Too many times we stand in God's way and our own way. I'm getting out of my own way. I want God to heal me, so I don't go through life limping. I intend on leaping with the purpose partner that I will be receiving.

THE NBA

Why would you expect God to bring your next, when you still haven't moved past the pain of your ex? Isn't that unfair to God, you, and your potential purpose partner too? Oftentimes, we treat relationships like it's the NBA. All we do is rebound. We expect the next person to deal with our pain from the last person. We expect them to ignore our insecurities and deal with our toxicity. Don't make the next one, pay for the mistake of the last one.

In many cases, we play ourselves in the National Broken Association because we have not taken the time to assist in our own healing. We want people to deal with our animosity, suspicions, fears, frailties, and preconceived notions that are impediments to longevity in relationships. The constant relationship rebounding, leads to further brokenness that blocks our blessings. Of course none of us are perfect, but what we bring to the table should be worth it.

MAKE IT "PLANE"

I love traveling, but I hate packing to fly the friendly skies. I realize when I check my luggage, that I have to pay more based upon how heavy the bag weighs. Whether the label on my bag says "Louis Vuitton" or "crouton" (that's the off brand), I still have to pay the fee. Realize that relationships are like boarding an airplane, too much baggage is going to cost you.

How many times, have you come across good looking people but you discovered they had a lot of ugly baggage? She looks pretty but her attitude is ugly. He looks handsome but he's a headache. Sometimes your baggage is as ugly as theirs too. It has cost you astronomically and immensely, to deal with the baggage of other people much less your own. You have to make it "plane" because you need who and what's right, if you're going to soar on your love flight. Based upon what you're carrying, it will cause you to crash into your past or soar into your future. If you're going to grow, you have to let it go. In order for the best to last, you have to forgive and let go of the unnecessary baggage from your past.

PEACE FROM BROKEN PIECES

I mentioned prior that one is a whole number, not a fraction. A fraction is part of a whole that has been reduced. It is part but not whole. So many times we live partly happy, partly committed, partly loving ourselves, and knowing our worth. Oftentimes we live on broken pieces.

We have a piece of our mind, but not peace of mind. We have been fractured by hurtful words, actions, abuse, insecurity, and misperceptions from society. The same fractured fragments of our lives, is what we bring into relationships with people who resemble the brokenness within ourselves. You literally become a magnet for the right one or the wrong one. You don't attract what you want. You attract who you are.

WHOLE OR HOLE?

Due to the feelings of incompleteness within us, we search for people and things to make us feel whole when we are just trying to fill a hole. We act out of emotion. We engage in emotional eating, emotional spending, and even step into relationships out of our emotions. Realize that emotions can wreck your life.

The love we are in search of becomes a mirage that holds us back. You will never benefit from the source, if all you do is go after resources. The love from God's heart, is more important than the luxuries that flow from His hand.

He is the only source that can fill and fulfill what is missing, damaged, and broken in your life. Sex won't fill it. Drugs, alcohol, and popping pills won't do it. Buying shoes, clothes, and cars can't satisfy it. Purchasing a house with your spouse won't sustain it. Suicide won't solve it. No amount of money, fame, or notoriety will ever fill what is only intended for God to fulfill. He can heal the hole in your heart, making you whole to give you a brand new start. When you walk in healing and wholeness, you will attract people who live in their greatness not brokenness.

ALONE BUT NOT LONELY

I heard someone say "It's better to be alone, than to be in the company of people who make you feel alone." Just because you're alone, doesn't mean you're lonely. It's further applied when you can enjoy your own company. If you can't stand to be alone with you, then why would anyone else want to be alone with you? Your excitement should begin within, not from them. You can't expect anybody to love you, if you don't love you. They can't make you happy, if you're not happy with yourself. You will still feel alone with them, if you don't know who you are apart from them.

Even the word "alone" has a suffix which is "one." You should strive to become one with God in a greater way. This is why they say, "The whole is greater than the sum of its parts." The break up, abuse, neglect, mistakes, trials, and times of defeat were only parts of your life. It's not the total sum of your life. I know you've heard, "Life is 10% what happens to you and 90% how you react to it." However, the deeper concept is that 90% of the time we focus on the 10%, where now the 10% becomes 100% of our lives. Rather than living in a state of wholeness, we walk in circles in a state of brokenness. You will never move forward, if you keep living your life in reverse. Leave the past in the past. You can't redo it. You have to live through it.

DATE OR WAIT?

In a place of singleness and solitude, is an opportunity to continue to grow and work on yourself. Many times we see it as delay or denial, when it's neither. God is orchestrating the right person and right opportunity, to collide with your destiny at the right timing. There are some goals and dreams, that God wants you to fulfill while you're single. Why wait to be married to do, what God wants you to do while you're single? As you're procrastinating, you're delaying your blessing.

It may not be your time to date, it just might be your time to wait. The context of "wait" doesn't mean to be idle. It means to continue moving, working, and preparing while you're expecting what you intend on receiving. You're not waiting on God, He's waiting on you. Brother, continue to work your vision and prepare your life for your wife. Sister, the right mister is looking for you and will find you walking

WIFE - DR. EDDIE CONNOR

in the purpose that God gave you. Even now, your future

purpose partner and supportive spouse is creating,

producing, building, and strategizing for something and

someone great.Will you meet them in your place of painful

brokenness or purposeful living through wholeness? Let

them find you, walking in the greatness within you.

CHAPTER 2

Who Can Find?

Before you look for them, find out who you are in Him.

One of the most promulgated passages of scripture, is found in Proverbs 31:10. The writer asked the question, "Who can find a virtuous woman? For her price is far above rubies." In essence, if I can buy her then she's not the one. It's interesting to note, rubies are found underground. Rubies are literally miles deep, below the ocean floor. A ruby is one of the most rare, royal, precious, and expensive jewels on the planet. The most expensive ruby to date, sold for an astounding rate of $57.5 million dollars. Yet the Bible affirms, that your value as a virtuous woman far exceeds that price.

In order to find a ruby, you literally have to dig for it

to get it. Sis, if a man is not willing to search for you and put in the work to get you, then he's not worthy of having you. Realize that your royalty demands loyalty. You're too unique to compete and too rare to compare. If he wants you, then he will approach you. A gentleman will become a gemologist, in order to find you.

VISION FOR DECISION

A man knows who and what he wants. A man knows when he wants to be around you and when he needs time alone. We may not always communicate and convey it, but please believe that we as men know what we want. We don't deal too much with duality, but we are decisive.

A man who doesn't know what he wants is dangerous. Scripture declares in James 1:8, "A double minded man is unstable in all his ways." Simply because indecision is a decision which affects the totality of your life, directly and indirectly. Brother, how can you expect to lead a woman if you don't know what you want, much less know where you're going? As men we need God's vision for our lives, in order to make wise decisions.

TIME SENSITIVE

As a woman, from the moment you were born, you've been hearing about this innate "biological clock" within. You matured faster mentally and physically, than the boys in your classroom. You may argue that we never caught up mentally. You began to notice at a young age, how your body operated in cycles according to a calendar. You planned the age of when you wanted to be married with children. Your prom was the prelude. You saw yourself in a wedding gown. You knew what ring you wanted, down to the exact color of the birthstone and carat size. We as men will never understand how you've always had it planned. By nature you have always been time sensitive. You're cautious and cognizant of time. You will even plan a detailed girl's trip, two years in advance. Your mind is never disconnected from the season and time because of your internal ticktock. By nature, you're a planner and time keeper. As a result, the last thing a woman wants a man to do, is to waste her time! Bro, don't play games with her time.

Please believe she's counted the hours, days, weeks, months, or even years that she's spent with you. She wants the relationship to be fruitful, instead of making her look pitiful for spending time that amounted to nothing. We as men are not always conscientious of your time. We know how much time is left in the quarter of a basketball game. We know how much time we have to put in, at the job each day. We know how long it will take us, to drive across town. We should also know the quality of time, when it comes to you.

Go and ask a married couple, how long they've been married. If a man knows, sometimes it's because he's mumbled when asked or been corrected enough to finally put it to memory. More often than not, a woman knows unequivocally how long she's been married or in a relationship with somebody.

Being time sensitive is not an excuse, to rush into what you want to last for a lifetime. A woman who is in a hurry relationally, can turn a man off entirely. One date doesn't constitute a relationship. There is a period of attaining data, to decide if you will remain as friends or date one another and pursue a relationship. Whatever you rush to get, you will have to move even faster to keep. A man who wants you, will not only convey it with words. It will be expressed in his deeds.

VICIOUS OR VIRTUOUS?

In Proverbs 31:10, the scripture never stated, "Who can find a voluptuous vixen?" It doesn't say, "Who can find a pretty face and a slim waist?" Beauty is only skin deep. It's fleeting and it fades. It will attract you, but there has to be more to keep you. Rather, you will find a virtuous woman, as the quality of person exemplified. In a world of quantity, a queen knows her value, worth, and quality. According to Proverbs 12:4, "A virtuous woman is a crown to her husband." She literally upgrades him. A man's life should be better, as a result of being connected to you. As his rib, he should breathe easier because of the crowning jewel that is you.

Are you vicious or virtuous, in the way that you carry yourself? Do your words have virtue? What is so unique about you that separates you from everyone else? Beyond you being exquisite on the outside, do you have beauty on the inside? A virtuous woman is desirable, unmistakable, highly capable, precious, and valuable. She operates in modesty, purity, and honesty. In a world of quantity, a woman of quality always stands out because she knows her value and worth.

FATEFUL OR FAITHFUL?

Proverbs 20:6 also affirms, "Who can find a faithful man?"
Many times we get Biblical amnesia, when it comes to this
particular verse about a faithful man. Maybe you're reading
this passage and didn't even know that verse existed. The
verse is not communicated, as much as Proverbs 31:10 is
promulgated. As a man are you faithful to God? Are you
faithful in your job/career? Are you faithful to being in your
son or daughter's life? Are you faithful to the commitments
you've made? If you're not faithful to God and the important
aspects of your life, then how can you expect to be faithful
to your future wife? We can't excuse our brokenness and
lack of accountability. There is no respectability without
responsibility. We extol the virtues and values of a woman
by expecting her to be faithful, pristine, and chaste. What
about us though? The same onus we place on women, is
rarely required to be upheld by men. When will we demand

more from ourselves, to uphold a standard as men?

KEEP IT 1,000

Imagine how powerful it would be, to communicate that loving your wife 1,000 ways, is more important than being with 1,000 women. What if that mode of thinking was the norm? It doesn't make you soft, less than a man or feminine. Respect and responsibility is the essence of true manhood and masculinity. Are women the only ones who need standards? How can we run through the streets, but expect our sisters to be saints? When we as men have standards and view ourselves as kings, then we will respect ourselves and our queens.

DOUBLE STANDARDS

The double standards in society are often extensions from within the home. Through the years I continue to hear, "We love our sons and raise our daughters." This conveys the challenge of how some parents spoil their sons, but are strict with their daughters. Think back to your childhood. As a boy raised with a sister(s), maybe there were opportunities that were extended to you which she could not enjoy. Maybe you were allowed to stay out later or could talk to girls, before she could talk to boys.

How can we ignore the glaring double standard. For instance, a guy can date an entire team of cheerleaders and be labeled "the man." However, if a girl dates more than one football player, she's labeled with an unsavory title. This emanates beyond the school into society.

As a girl being raised alongside your brother(s), think about the things they were able to get away with, that you would always get in trouble over. Maybe you cooked and they didn't have to learn how to. Maybe you ironed their clothes, did their homework, or even allowed them to cheat off your paper. Maybe you were even disciplined for not keeping your brothers in line, when they were supposed to behave on their own. When you excelled in academics it was because you were supposed to. When we came home with a few good grades as boys, they just about threw a party. You were raised, but we were loved. Too often we coddle our boys, to be raised with a sense of entitlement.

Yes, the restrictions are all in the name of protecting our girls from perpetrators and raising them to be great wives and mothers. However, was that same onus placed on us as boys, to be great husbands and fathers? Did we prepare women for unprepared men? We know how to plant the seed, but did anyone teach us to tend the soil? What happens when a woman who was raised to be disciplined, falls in love with a man who is impulsive? When you consider the fact that she was raised but he was loved, herein lies the conflict.

Sometimes mothers in their anger and disappointment, communicate to our girls that they don't need a man. So they are raised to be independent not interdependent. As a result, even our boys internalize their mother's disappointment.

They hear how their sister doesn't need a man and consequently, they don't want to become a man. If being a "man" means I'm not present, what does that communicate? I rarely if ever see you. I don't have a relationship with you. I have not learned anything, but how to be the opposite of you. Why would I want to become a "man" just like you? Why would I want to be what disappointed me? Therefore, it's easier for us to live feeling entitled and void of vision, as "grown boys" because of what we have internalized as young boys.

MALE VS. MAN

Just because you're a male, doesn't mean you're a man. A male is someone who operates in their gender aimlessly. A man is one who leads and lives, respectfully and responsibly. As a man, there is no respectability without responsibility. What is your response in the community, school system, home, with your children, gifts, talents, relationships, and career? Being a man is not about what you possess below the waist. It's about what you possess above the neck. When was the last time you took pride in using your mind, as you do your muscles?

KNOW THAT YOU "NO"

Due to the differences in how we were raised, women are generally taught to say "no." You came into the awareness of your body and even how desirable you would eventually become. So you're trained to say "no," but not trained to hear "no." As men we were trained to hear "no," but we were not trained to say "no." So what happens when someone who was not trained to hear "no," makes a move on someone who was not trained to say "no?"

Hypothetically, if a man turns down your beautiful voluptuous pulchritude, amidst your flirtation, then what is your initial thought? Since you're not used to men turning you down, maybe you get on the phone with your girlfriend and question the man's sexuality. Something has to be wrong with him, if he doesn't want you. Now, why couldn't the man just love Jesus? Why can't he be someone whose trying to live holy, have a standard, and strive to be celibate? If he approaches you and you're not interested then he's "too thirsty." However, if he turns you down, do you question his sexual orientation? Oftentimes, there is a double standard because of how we were raised and socialized. As men we are taught to conquer and be competitive, but not to be compassionate and committed. So much so, that when we strive to become the latter, we are seen as an anomaly with an assault on our masculinity.

ANSWERING THE QUESTION

There are so many variables to relationships, dating, and marriage that the writer in Proverbs 20:6 and Proverbs 31:10 asked the foundational question, "Who can find?" It's a question that is rhetorical yet powerful. For the writer to include that assertion, means there's little supply and great demand. Gospel singer, VaShawn Mitchell would say, "I've searched all over, couldn't find nobody. I looked high and low, still couldn't find nobody." Simply because quantity is everywhere, but quality is rare.

There is a quantity of men and women, but not all are quality men and women. The writer also knows, that we are choosing out of flawed and broken mechanics. Our proclivities and tendencies often cloud our judgment. If it's not in a certain package, many of us will avoid it. We have a predilection, for the particular type of person we desire.

Could it be that your "type" is the reason why you're single? Might I suggest, that the reason you continue to be hurt is because of the type of person you choose. Sometimes what we choose, is not always the best choice for us. Don't get so lost in desire and attraction, at the expense of losing integrity and affection. Your type might be temporary, but your prototype is permanent.

In this life, we all live to be chosen. You want to be chosen to play on the team. You want to be chosen for the promotion. We want our name chosen to win a prize. We want the right person, to choose to love us because of who we are not for what we have. Spiritually, you are chosen by God to do great things. Ephesians 1:4 declares, "We are chosen in Him before the foundation of the world."

We live to be chosen. The power of selection is key but the power of being selective, opens the right door with that key. You have to allow God to guide you as a man, to find a virtuous woman. He also has to guide you as a woman, to be found by the right man who is faithful. You can't expect a man to be faithful to you, if he is not first faithful to God.

HEALED TO FIND

Never go into a relationship, if you're not healed. You will always make bad choices, when you choose from weakness rather than strength. Don't choose somebody to change them. You can't change anybody. Only God can do that. If they are not what you want, don't waste your time and energy trying to make someone become what you want them to be. On the contrary, sometimes what you want is not what you need. It will never be the right time, if it's the wrong person. Don't rush into, what you will end up regretting. You never want to lower your standards, just for the sake of having somebody. Aspire to be the best, attain the best, and settle for nothing less.

Oftentimes because we have been hurt, broken, and disappointed we now lower our level of expectation. Nothing is worse, than when your expectation and experience don't align. What you expected someone to be, was not who you experienced when you got to know them. As a result, we stop seeking the best and settle for the worst. So often people become serial daters. They move from relationship to relationship, taking old baggage into new relationships.

Are you complaining, comparing, and crying or positioning yourself to be found as a wife? Are you preparing yourself to do the finding as a husband? The positioning and preparing comes through the process of healing. It comes through the process of taking time to be alone. It is ingrained in removing the mask of your past and dealing with issues that you've tried to cover. It eliminates self-destructive behaviors, that cloud your conscience and place you in a greater cesspool of low self-esteem. The process leads to progress, when we allow God into the places of our lives that were deemed untouchable. Without taking the time to heal, the scars of your past will continue to last.

IS YOUR HOUSE A HOME?

Why expect God to send your spouse, when there still needs to be healing in your house? The house is not only what you've furnished and the number of bedrooms, in your living space. It's not solely where you reside, but what resides in you. The house is you. The skeletons in your closet that you haven't addressed. The messy rooms of your past, that you shut the door on and won't allow God access into. The house is your mind, will, and emotions of what takes place internally.

Is your house a home? Is there chaos or peace in your house? So many times we look for people to clean up and fix what is wrong with us, when that job belongs to God. Everybody doesn't want love, some just want help. People with problems of their own can't solve ours. Only God who is the problem solver can do that. Before you look for them, find out who you are in Him. When you stop searching for just anything, you will begin finding everything in God.

CHAPTER 3

Purpose Partner

The right one for you, will walk by faith with you,
into the purpose God gave you.

I recall hearing the quote "A job is what you're paid for, but your purpose is what you're made for." Do you know your purpose for being on this planet? Beyond a job, spouse, house, children, cars, clothes, and valuable possessions. Do you know your value within, that propels you into purposeful living? Oftentimes, we think our value is connected to what we do, where we live, or drive. However, it's rooted in who you are. You can never truly know who you are, until you know whose you are. Realize that you are a child of God. Your royalty is aligned with your destiny, to think and live on a greater frequency.

PURPOSE DRIVEN LIVING

Realize as long as you have a pulse, you have a purpose. What you've been through doesn't disqualify you. In fact it validates you because you made it through, what was designed to destroy you. There is a purpose through your process. A message despite your mess and a testimony coming out of your test. You must realize that you are alive on purpose and for a purpose, because you have a dynamic purpose.

WHAT IS YOUR WHY?

There is an African proverb that suggests, "The two most important dates in your life, is the day you were born and the day you realize why you were born." The day you were born is indeed a celebration of life, but the day you realize why you were born is an elevation of your life. The awakening within you elevates your mind, body, spirit, and purpose. The fact that you were born is an event in a geographical location. Yet in juxtaposition, the discovery of why you were born is an awakening spiritually and psychologically, throughout the parameters of your mind. When you realize why you were born, it gives you power to move in the magnanimity of your purpose. When you understand why you were born, it transitions you from merely existing in life, to living on purpose for life.

There are some people in your life, that don't fit your purpose. I have grown to understand that for some people, their only purpose in life is to distract you from fulfilling your purpose. Don't let anybody become an impediment to your success and don't get in the way of your own either. Sometimes we can be our worst enemies and get in our own way. In that instance, the greatest enemy is sometimes the inner me. However, when you're focused, resilient, and determined you will eventually become an asset to yourself.

GROW TO GO

In a world of ordinary people, there is something extraordinary about you. Realize that you are at a prime location in your life, because you are at the intersection of preparation and opportunity. Everything that you've been through, has prepared you for the next level. Don't let negative experiences stop you. Don't allow your mistakes to minimize you. Learn how to handle the negative, positively. It's not only about what you go through, because we all go through something in life. It's more about how you grow through, what you go through. Your purpose should compel and propel you to persevere.

LEVEL UP

What you're thinking will dictate where you're going. For you to get to the next level, you have to lift your mind to a greater level. Oftentimes, the greatest impediment to our success is our mindset. If you're thinking negative, that is exactly what the result will be. If you think little of yourself, you will do little for yourself and others. Replace procrastination and mental discombobulation with determination. Press past the negative and move into a place of positivity. Read something that will empower you. Listen to something that will encourage you and place yourself in the company of those who will inspire you. Each day, take steps to lift your mind and purpose to another level.

Next level living, comes as a result of leaving your past in the past. I've learned that people will bring up your past, because they have no power to stop your future. You have the power to change your future, but it's powerless if you live in the past. Let every hurt go, let negative people go, and begin to grow through pain. Learn from your past, don't live in it. Don't let your past imprison your future. The past is a prison, but your future is freedom. Blast past your past, recommit to the present, and plan for the future. This is not the time to break down. This is your time to break through. Release the past, rejoice in the present, and reach for the future. Don't let anything divide you from your destiny or subtract from your success. Your future is far greater than your past!

LOCALLY AND GLOBALLY

Could it be that God has a great work for you to do, locally or even globally before you connect with your spouse? Maybe your work is the vehicle, that will connect you with your purpose partner. How will you know if you don't harness your talent, stir up your gifts, get active, grow, and go? You have to be in the right place and in the right position, to make the connection with the right person.

Realize that you are gifted and mandated, to contribute your gifts to empower others. Wherever you are planted, bloom there. Nurture, develop, and enhance your gifts to enrich lives and your community. What are you passionate about? What are you driven to do and pursue?

There is a solution that you can provide to the problems that your community, school, or government is facing. Begin to think critically, to find a remedy to the malady that you're passionate about. There is a gift in you that can bless the world. Start where you are. The harvest is abundant but the laborers are scarce. Your gift will make room for you. Develop your gift. It can take you from the most remote places on the planet, to the most prominent platforms. When you impact people locally, you will be in a position to do greater things globally.

LIMPING TO LEAPING

Don't be afraid to do something different. Doing the same thing, expecting a different result will only yield the same result. Lifting your mind to the next level, empowers you to leap into the stratosphere of success. Don't say it won't work, if you haven't tried it. Even if you've tried, try it again. So many times, we have allowed people to cripple us and reduce our big ideas. These factors fracture us, by leaving us limping rather than leaping into our destiny. Lift your mind above what limited you. Take the leap and believe that all things are possible. Your faith is like a muscle, it strengthens when you stretch it. Leap, stretch, and move to the next level!

Remember there are three types of people in life: those who wait for it to happen, those who let it happen, and those who have the tenacity to make it happen! Which one are you? If no one ever gives you an opportunity, then use your gifts to create an opportunity. Go for it! You're too close to quit. Don't give up on your dreams. Shake off the negativity and move into opportunity, by walking in your purpose! Live with purpose. Live for a purpose. Leap into your purpose.

RUNNING MATE

Be confident in knowing that God will bless you with

someone to run with, not run from. Realize the right one for you is tailor-made, to be a suitable asset and partner to you. The right one for you, is qualified to run with the vision that God gave you. They will be in sync and in step. When you move they will move just like that. You won't have to drag the right one for you, to be with you. They will move their feet on beat and in sync with you. Stay prayerful and run your race with patience. Your purpose partner will literally be your running mate.

On your path to purpose, God will connect you with the right one to finish the race as one. The victory is already won. Remember where God guides, He always provides. As your hearts are connected, run hand in hand with your purpose partner toward the vision. You will attain provision. If you wait on God, He will order your steps to run with the right one, so you won't run from the wrong one.

POWER COUPLE VS. PURPOSE PARTNER

I know you can easily find a partner, but most importantly you need a purpose partner. A purpose partner is a teammate not an opponent. They are an asset in love to you, to fulfill the plan and purpose that God has for you. We have become so inundated by the term "power couple." Many people want a love connection, like their favorite celebrity relationships or marriages. You see the lights, cameras, wealth, acclaim, and fame but you truly don't know what goes on behind the scenes. We fall in love with imagery, but what is your personal strategy? Sometimes the term "power couple" means power struggle. The right one will strengthen you. They will empower you to walk in your purpose, as your purpose partner.

In order to receive a purpose partner, you first have to know your purpose. You also have to walk in that purpose and execute by using your gifts. Beyond the title of "purpose partner" you have to possess the nature of a purpose partner. God's love, compassion, commitment, character, ambition, introspection, and the desire to grow are key qualities. A purpose partner will not fulfill your purpose for you. They will fulfill it with you. Some people can't grow and build with you, because they're intimidated by you. Remember whoever you intimidate, is who you will eliminate. Let them go and don't look back.

Beyond someone looking good to you, are they good for you? Don't let what attracts you, ultimately distract you from recognizing who values you. Let God lead you to discern who He has for you. Realize that your purpose partner will bring peace not pressure. They will bring compatibility and suitability not anxiety.

TIMING IS EVERYTHING

So many times people compare themselves to others. They ask when will their time for love, meeting the right one, and building with their purpose partner come? As a result, we find ourselves in a hurry going nowhere. Rushing and ruining it all at the same time. Have we lost sight of the virtue of patience? Ecclesiastes 3:1 declares, "To everything there is a season and a time to every purpose under the heaven." In essence, timing is everything.

You have a date with destiny. Before partnering, make sure that your steps are ordered via purposeful living. You're anointed for your appointed time. God can give you the desires of your heart suddenly, as you walk faithfully. Don't focus on the destination more than the journey. Every step is a necessary component toward the fulfillment of the blessing.

WORTH THE WAIT

Do you only want what you want or do you want what God has for you? Most of the time, what we want is not what we need. It's temporary but not permanent. The time and season

Autumn,

May this trip
be filled w/ many
thngs for you!
Good food! Laughtr
memories & breath
taking moments

May 2019 Be a
consistant reminder
of who God is.
Faithful!

& as we prep for 2020
May you know the
Best is yet to
come for you + yours

For God so loved the world, that he gave his only begotten Son, that whosoever believeth in him should not perish, but have everlasting life.
John 3:16

12/14/18

of your life, must align with the purpose that God has for your life. Realize what God is preparing is worth you waiting. You're worth the wait and so is the blessing that God has for you. Don't allow people to rush you. Don't allow a stigma to offset you. Don't allow people's perceptions of you, to make you pursue what isn't aligned with the purpose that God has for you. It's better to wait long than to settle for what's wrong. While you're waiting, keep working and God will provide the blessing. In due time, your life will connect with the purpose partner that He has for you.

Take the time to grow your gifts and develop your dreams as you're waiting. What you're expecting is not delayed or denied. It will happen at the right time. Learn how to stand still and let God reveal who He has for you. Realize that God can satisfy the hunger in your soul, even in your singleness. Align yourself in relationship with God through His Word. You will see greater works that come to fruition in your life.

ALL OR NOTHING

So often, we give all of ourselves to people but only pieces of ourselves to God. How many times have you given your all to someone, only to receive nothing in return? You gave your heart, time, money, energy, and even your body but were still broken internally. The hurt you received in exchange for what you gave wasn't worth it. What if you gave your all to Him, just like you gave your all to the them?

God doesn't want a fragmented friendship or a part-time partnership with you. He doesn't want a lukewarm and tepid experience. He wants you to be on fire for Him. Totally committed and submitted to His will for your life. God wants all of your trust, devotion, and yes even pain. Give Him your frustration and He will give you faith. Give Him your pain and He will give you power.

People will easily throw you away, for your mistakes

or lack of measuring up to their approval of you. However, despite your mistakes and missteps, God still extends His love toward you. His forgiveness and grace is still granted without hesitation. If you give all of yourself to Him, then you won't have to chase them. You won't have to search for the wrong people to love you, because you're void of self-love. When God is your source, you will have the resources. He will provide you with all things, even when you have nothing at all.

WHAT ARE YOU THIRSTING FOR?

When you're thirsty for the wrong thing, you will end up accepting and settling for anything. When you're dissatisfied you surround yourself with different bodies, to make you feel like somebody. You really need love but you will settle for sex, in hopes that your thirst can be quenched. You will always be empty, looking for someone to fill your void.

A need that's left unaddressed is dangerous. A need

will make you operate out of desperation. When they say, "Desperate times call for desperate measures" they didn't lie. People who are needy will go to desperate measures and great lengths, because of the intensity of their thirst. When you're needy and thirsty, you will settle but never get to the next level. You don't have to lower your standards, for the sake of having somebody. A person cannot fill the void in your life or make you happy, if you're not happy with yourself. When you're not happy, you can't make anybody else happy. You can't give anybody anything that you don't have. If you're void of love or affirmation, you can't give it. In most cases, you will refuse to receive it because of how you've been treated.

Have you ever considered that God can satisfy you? Deep within, do you really believe that He can? God can take the messy, broken, and wounded issues in your life, by blessing, touching, and healing you from every infirmity. Whether you're alone or in a one bedroom apartment, He can satisfy you. For all of the people who disappointed you, God is getting ready to surprise and satisfy you. He will empower you, so that the joy of the Lord is your strength.

A man, woman, money, career, cars, clothes, and possessions will pacify you, but it won't satisfy you. When you thirst for the wrong things, you end up parched if not dehydrated. Just like the woman at the well in John 4, only Jesus can quench your thirsty soul. The spiritual satisfaction that He places in your soul, will make you look at your situation and declare all is well. God will make you whole. When you feel depressed, desperate, or in a drought, the well of God's living water will spring up within you. The living water of the Lord, will refresh and satisfy your thirsty soul.

ACCESS GRANTED

Allow God into the cracks and crevices of your life. Yes, even the secret places that have been so painful, to where you wouldn't even utter a word. Allow Him access. Too often we make the mistake of only allowing God access into certain places of our lives, that He knows about anyway. Jesus declared, "Behold I stand at the door and knock" (Revelation 3:20). He will not break down or pick the lock on the door. You have to willingly open the door of your heart, mind, relationships, and past. Don't grant access to people, but deny access to God. Proverbs 3:5, 6 affirms, "Trust in the Lord with all thine heart and lean not unto thine own understanding. In all thy ways acknowledge Him and He shall direct thy paths." When you lean to your own understanding you will fall. Only when you allow God access to guide you, then you can stand tall.

THANKS BUT NO THANKS

Many times we don't want to trust God, rather we want to help God. He doesn't need your help. Nothing is new to God. He is omniscient, so He never receives any new information. Let go and let God handle it. Let Him provide your purpose partner. Let Him sustain you, in your time of singleness by being selective. Stop stressing and start trusting.

Have you ever had someone offer their help to assist you with a particular task, but they were a headache and a hindrance? They were not in sync with you. They didn't have prior knowledge and really were no help at all. So much so that you just said, "Thanks but not thanks. I got this." You took longer to complete it, because they got in the way of it. How many times have you delayed what God has for you, by getting in the way of what He's prepared for you? Does God have to tell you to move and get out of the way? Maybe He already told you. Try helping yourself out, by deciding not to help God out. He doesn't need it. Take your hands off it and let Him handle it. Walk by faith and not by sight into it. God is working on things for you and He's also working on you too. Just breathe and believe. The blessing is already yours to receive.

PURPOSE ON PURPOSE

The next relationship that you embark on will be God ordained, aligned, and designed. Know that everything you've been through was only preparing you, for what God has for you. It's for a purpose because you are being connected, with the right partner on purpose. You will walk by faith, with your purpose partner and run with the vision in the right direction. You're about to enter a relationship that only God, can get the credit for it. This time the tears you shed will be those of joy. The shout won't be one of anxiety, but of opportunity. The testimony will erase the past memories. Yes, you will be glad to have them, but you will still give glory to Him. The fulfillment of the promise is worth the process. Even the wrong one, was a setup for the right one.

IT'S ALL GOOD

Romans 8:28 encourages you to know, "All things work

together for good to them that love God, to them who are the

called according to His purpose." Through your journey of

love, loss, trials, triumphs, setbacks, and comebacks you will

still say "It's all good." They didn't see your value, but it's

all good. The struggle made you stronger, so it's all good.

The rejection was redirection, so it's all good. God is

currently preparing you, for the purpose partner that He has

for you. Whatever you go through, know that something

good will come from it for you. So rise above it. The reason

it's all good because it's all God!

Prepare for the right one that God has for you. They

will thank God for you and with you. More than who you

know or who introduced who, God is the one who arranged

it for you. Move out of the way and watch how things work

out in every way. Take your hands off it and let God develop

it. Your purpose partner won't compete with you. They will

bring out the best in you. They will collaborate to execute

the vision God gave you. When people see you with your

purpose partner, they will shake their head in amazement

and won't get it, but God will get the credit!

CHAPTER 4

Why Would I Get Married?

Love is not about finding a person who is perfect,
but someone who is worth it.

In 2007, actor and filmmaker Tyler Perry brought to the silver screen, *Why Did I Get Married?* This particular movie, unveiled the ups and downs in love, life, and relationships, within the matrix of marriage.

Researchers suggest that more than 50% of all marriages end in divorce. Indeed the institution of marriage is under attack and in the crosshairs of our country. As a caveat, the divorce rate is higher in the church than it is among the secular culture. Some may say, "If people who are Bible-toting believers can't keep it together, then why would the people in the world want to walk down the aisle?"

Is it too risky to marry?

MARRED MARRIAGE

The issues of marriage and divorce, may even make Tyler Perry think of writing another movie, *Why Would I Get Married*? I wouldn't mind making a cameo appearance. I say that sarcastically, yet seriously because of an alarming study about dating, relationships, and marriage in recent years. According to a Pew Research study, 40% of Americans say there is no need for marriage. How do you plan for the future, with someone who doesn't see marriage in their future?

It seems as if there is a growing subculture of individuals, who are choosing to be single for life, by "abstaining from marriage." Some would rather cohabit (my grandmother would call it "shacking up") or engage in long-term dating. Some view being single to be more financially feasible. Others are still feeling the sting of bad relationship experiences. Are these valid reasons to not walk down the aisle? What if you didn't grow up in a household with a strong marriage example? Could that impact your decision to marry?

I personally grew up in a divorced home, being raised by my mother. Without a doubt, divorce or an absentee parent will shape any person's view of relationships. As a result, your outlook on marriage can be juxtaposed ambivalently and optimistically.

Undoubtedly, as we look around our communities, we can see that we are a generation of fatherless sons and daddyless daughters. Our families are broken.

The idea of love has become some foreign, alien, and mystical word to many of us in a number of ways. To a certain degree, it's as if you reach for it but you can't grasp it. Love has often never been experienced. It required us to give up something or it was connected to a lot of pain. If it was promulgated to you in that way, then it wasn't real love.

FACTS VS. TRUTH

Sigmund Freud, the father of psychoanalysis, suggested "Childhood experiences shape our personalities and behavior as adults." Freud's rationale is that we can be no better than our childhood development, due to what we have been exposed to.

A noted psychologist, Francis Galton, coined the phrase and developed the concept of *Nature vs. Nurture.* The abstract idea is immersed in the fact, that it's not always who we are but how we have been raised. Our environments and interactions play a significant factor in our lives.

The substratum of *Nature,* underscores the fact that genetics and natural influences shape one's behavior and decision making. On the contrary, *Nurture* argues that a person develops through the influences of people, experiences, and interactions to formulate one's life. In essence, is the totality of who you are innate or is it learned through experience?

I'm a living witness, that you can have the facts and still not have the truth. The fact is that your past impacts your life. The truth is that you are not your past or the sum of your experiences. Your situation does not define you, unless you allow it to. You have the power to define your situation. Yes, you may have been hurt, but you can still discover the power of healing and love despite pain.

You may say, "I have only experienced hurt, pain, mistrust, and unhappiness. How can I embrace love from God? Will He let me down like everyone else? How can I embrace what I have never experienced?" Many times we bag, box, and bring our brokenness into new relationships. However, they never become fruitful because we have not rid ourselves of the vestiges of our past.

GOING IN CIRCLES

Yes, you're delivered but have you been healed? You may not be in the situation that brought the pain, but your mind and heart are still battling with the pain. Physically you may be free but psychologically, spiritually, and emotionally there is still brokenness within. I recall telling someone my story, of grappling and gaining victory over cancer. I told them "Although I'm healed, I wasn't healed." For many years post cancer, the psychological and emotional scars had a grip on my life. Healing is not an overnight instance, it's a continual process. When you begin to trust God and experience His love, there will be healing that flows through your life. God will show you how to love yourself and as a result, love others.

If you live your life going in circles, you will never make substantial progress. You must use every breaking point, to break free from the circumstances that seek to break you down. Break free from the whirlwinds of worry and the tornados of trials and tribulations. When you begin to break the cycle, you will experience love under new management.

THE NEW IS NOW

Old mindsets and lifestyles, must be replaced by new levels of thinking and living. Your mind is like a computer that stores information and can be used as a resource, to connect to your world. You can't run new software on an old computer. Much like new ideas aren't made for old mindsets.

What is on your mental hard drive and what are you downloading into your mind? You can't live positively, if you're thinking negatively. The laws of sowing and reaping have always been true. You can't plant orange seeds and reap apples. The same is true for your life. What you sow will grow. The seeds that you plant on the inside, will manifest into trees of truth or weeds of worry on the outside.

God is the conduit by which love under new management is experienced. There is unity but also a deep divide between God's love and His law. The cross and the commandments. Religion and relationship. Law denotes, if you break the commandment you die. On the contrary, love affirms that you broke the commandment. However, despite your weaknesses, God's grace is sufficient (II Corinthians 12:9).

Grace is the bridge that merges God's law and His love. So if I am out of fellowship, our love relationship can and will be restored. You're not so far gone that His love can't pull you back. Religion says, "If I obey, God will love me." Relationship says, "Because God loves me, I can obey." John 4:24 declares, "For God is a Spirit and they that worship Him, must worship Him in spirit and in truth." There is no way that you can revere and worship, what you don't love. You can't worship in truth, if you're living a lie.

There are distinctive differences between the Old and New Testament. One is that the Old Testament, places an emphasis on the fear or reverence of God. On the other hand, the New Testament emphasizes the love of God. If you have experienced God's love and it lives within you, it now becomes the ebb and flow of life expressed in your

relationships.

U AND I

Within the matrix of relationships, there must be solid

communication if you intend for it to flourish. There is no

way that you can spell *communication*, without *"u"* and *"i"*

in proximity. It takes a committed tandem and teamwork to

communicate. The building block of communication is the

foundational framework, for the development of that

relationship. Good communication is necessary whether in

business, dating, or marriage. A lack of communication can

suffocate a relationship, but good communication can

breathe life into it. One of our biggest communication

mistakes is when we listen to reply, instead of listening to

understand. Listening is not waiting to talk!

As men and women communicate, we must

understand that the essence of communication is not solely

about your ability to speak. It's more importantly about your ability to listen. It's not only about what you say. It's how you listen to what is being said. Communication and comprehension are essential components to relational compatibility.

MARS VS. VENUS

Growing up I would hear people say, "Men are from Mars and women are from Venus." This statement underscores the differences between men and women, who seem to be from two different planets. Yes, it may feel that way at times, but the benefits outweigh the frustrations. Maybe a deeper description, is that men are like waffles and women are like spaghetti.

Here is what I mean. As men we have our categories for things and we generally don't intertwine everything together. We will compartmentalize our lives and often separate facts from feelings. Much like spaghetti, women have a propensity to mix, intertwine, and merge everything together.

For instance, ask a woman how was her day. Go ahead and ask. I guarantee she will tell you how it was from 5:30 a.m., when she woke up and put her feet in her slippers, until the time at 11:00 p.m., when she intends to wrap her hair for the night. Her explanation will be descriptive and in detailed depth. She will express her feelings about the occurrences of the day. Indeed there is truth and humor in the way we communicate.

On the other hand, try asking a man how was his day. He will generally say, "It was good." Now some men may give you a little more information, often from proposed questions. However, in all sincerity it was a good day for him. The facts about his day will generally be conveyed, more than his feelings about that day.

A woman will express how she felt and render the details. A man is going to give you the facts and figures. Just because men and women are different, doesn't mean that a specific gender is deficient. Both men and women are communicative beings. We just express ourselves differently, via verbal and nonverbal methods of communication.

Four of the most frightening words to a man, is when a woman says, "We need to talk." As men we generally don't like to talk. For one thing, we know we can't out argue you. We also know that you remember everything. Much like a filing cabinet, you know which folder to choose when you need to choose it. Your mind is incomparable. As men, we know how to talk about how fine a woman looks. We know how to talk about our favorite athletes and sports teams. We know how to talk about how much money we make. However, we don't often know how to communicate what we feel. We've been taught to repress instead of address, confess, and express.

WHAT'S IN YOUR BANK?

Whether you know it or not, everyone has a daily word bank. Communication researchers suggest, that men on average use 10,000 words a day (5,000 words at their specific place of employment). Women use approximately 20,000 words each day (10,000 words at their place of employment). So, let's analyze this word bank. When a husband and wife leave their respective jobs/careers and come home, generally there is a mathematical gap in communication.

For instance, they each arrive at home in their "his and hers Mercedes Benz" and take time to relax. In doing so, now the conversation begins about the day and their relationship. So the man uses his remaining 5,000 words during the conversation. Keep in mind, that he has now depleted his word bank. The woman still has another 10,000 words, left in her bank.

So think about it, now the man is out of conversation and the woman is still communicating. Have you ever experienced this? If so, what side were you on in the conversation? Now she's saying to him, "Why don't you talk to me?" He's thinking, "I don't have anything to say." Little does she know, that he used up all of the words in his bank.

Now brother if she says to you, "Why am I the only one talking?" Now you can tell her, "I've used all of the words in my bank for the day!" Sis, I'm sure you're thinking, "If he's smart he will borrow words from my bank, use some on credit, and keep the conversation going." Yes, with three snaps and a neck roll included. As funny as it sounds, oftentimes men and women clash, because of communication differences or simply the lack of understanding one another.

LISTEN AND SILENT

For any relationship to have success, you have to talk but you also have to listen. Both are intertwined in the art of communication. I believe that women are the stronger communicative beings. The ability to communicate can be an asset, as opposed to a liability when used carefully.

Do you have the composure to listen and hear, beyond what your eyes can only see? Don't just listen to what people say. Listen to what they are not saying. It takes discipline to listen and be silent. It's interesting that the words "listen" and "silent" have the same letters. Yet both are priceless words. Our words are like swords, that can cut someone or sharpen them. We must use them wisely as we communicate daily.

The immersion of communication and feelings, is what makes women highly resourceful and compassionate nurturers. On many occasions when I was a child, I witnessed my mother create something out of nothing. Many women today, also possess the power to do the same. It must be harnessed to heal rather than hurt others.

LIKE, LOVE, LUST

You don't need a TV sitcom, to tell you that it's *A Different World.* Just look around and recognize the signs of the times.

Back in the day, people would make a point to get to know you, before they "got to know you" if you know what I'm saying.

Like, love, and lust are seemingly indistinguishable for people. Oftentimes, we make the mistake of confusing the three. It generally happens when you look for love externally, before developing it internally. When you become a person of love, you will begin to attract real love that's selfless. Not lust which is selfish.

We are living in a generation where outward beauty can be bought, alternative facts are the new truth, and love is a foreign language. It's foreign because LOVE has sadly been defined as, "Legs Open Very Easily."

We are not living in The Victorian Era of sexual restraint and morality. Our culture has become overtly sexualized, to where lust is the new language. Understand that love doesn't play games with you. It doesn't seek to take or perpetuate negativity upon you. Love doesn't pawn or pimp you. Love doesn't bring confusion, it brings clarity. Lust and like won't lead you to love. Only God's love letter will do that.

Many times our hearts have been broken and bruised, by people who mishandled love. They masqueraded it via like and lust. As a result, we have emotionally, psychologically, and spiritually filed for love bankruptcy.

LOVE LETTER

I Corinthians 13 grants us a love letter conveying, "Love is patient, love is kind. Love does not envy or keep a record of wrongs." The passage affirms, that you can be intoxicated with the exuberance of your intellectual verbosity, to where you speak with royal eloquence and angelic ecstasy.

However, if you're a hateful, bitter, mean, and ruthless person it means nothing. In essence, you simply sound like the irritating noise of a rusty gate, or a squeaky door in need of WD-40. Only the oil of God's anointing, can flush out anger, bitterness, and strife in your life. When love flows through your heart, you're quick to forgive and slow to criticize.

When you express that you love something or someone, what does it really mean? How do you define love? In relationships, it's worth asking, "Do I love you the way I think you should be loved or do I love you, the way you need to be loved?"

As a human being with limitations and frailties, can you love someone unconditionally? Think about that for a minute. Do you have the capacity, to love without limits and conditions? I would suggest, emphatically no.

The finite frailty of human love comes with conditions and restrictions. If you transgress, you can be exiled and terminated from someone's life. However, God's love is unconditional. You can't out-evil God's goodness and love. However, He commands us to exemplify and express love to each other, even through our flawed mechanics.

Every relationship has a deal breaker. If it's not communicated and expressed, it is thought about. There are some things you can tolerate, but other things are intolerable. The only one, who can love without limits and express love unconditionally is God.

You can have the intent to love, but it must entail the extent that goes beyond finite limitations. The more connected we are to God, the more His love is able to flow in and through us. As a result, we can look beyond the conditions of others, to embrace their needs. If God looked beyond your faults and saw your needs, then surely you can do the same for someone else.

THE ULTIMATE GIFT

Many times we give gifts to express our love, appreciation, or engender someone's interest in us. Eventually the gifts get old, break, and fade into a distant memory. I've come to the realization that love is the only gift, that you can keep giving and never run out of it. Love is the ultimate gift that keeps on giving. Tangible gifts don't replace love, because love is the greatest gift. You may be alone, but it doesn't mean that you have to be lonely. God has never left you and He placed love within your heart. You can never expect anyone to love you, until you start loving yourself.

Eugene Peterson declared, "The person who refuses to love, doesn't know the first thing about God because God is love. You can't know Him, if you don't love." In essence, I can't love God, if I don't know God. I also can't know God, if I don't love Him. When you know His love for you, it makes you love Him back and show love to someone else. Knowing God's love, gives you self-love and self-love births a love for others.

God's love is too high for you to climb over it. So wide that you can't go around it. His love is rooted so deep, that you can't go under it. He just wants you to step into it. You can't be worse than His best. You can't be more evil than His goodness. You can't hate more than He loves.

God's love is like GPS. He finds us in our mess and makes

our   destination a great message. Only God can find you,

where everyone else left you. He will rescue and give you

relief.

BLAST PAST YOUR PAST

You can't marry your future, until you divorce your past.

There is no denying the fact that everyone has a past. How

much of someone's past, is too much to bring into your

future? Real love is not about finding a person who is

perfect, but someone who is worth it. Love is not a taker.

Love is a giver. Love understands that it's not about what

you have. It's about who you are and whose you are.

Recognize that you are God's child and you are deserving

of love. You can't be bought or sold. You're priceless. Gifts

don't replace love, for love is the greatest gift. When you

look through the lens of love, beyond someone's past, you

will see that it's about their heart not the way they start.

HEAL BEFORE YOU DEAL

My mother, Dr. Janice Connor, spoke at a conference on inner-healing, forgiveness, and purpose. She told the attendees that "Healing begins in the heart, when one is ready to dissect the root cause of pain." While she was speaking, I was meditating on her aphorism and making important connections to my own life.

There are certain words and statements that hit home to your heart, in order to heal you before you deal with someone new. You can't show love with bitterness and hatred in your heart. Real love will bring healing, to every wound in your life.

Some people hate the truth and fall in love with a lie. God will love you with the evidence, when people will hate you based on speculation. Dr. Martin Luther King, Jr. declared, "Hate cannot drive out hate, only love can do that." You should be too busy showing love, to hate someone else. You can't love anyone, until you first love God and yourself.

IS IT LOVE OR LIP SERVICE?

You don't need phony, fair-weather friends, and fickle folks in your life. You need dependability and sustainability. How someone treats you, is an indication of who they are and what you allow. Realize that you give people a blueprint on how to treat you, by the way you treat yourself. Sometimes you have to teach people how to treat you, or they will mistreat you. The substratum of how they treat you, is also an indication of what they think about themselves. If they don't think much of themselves, they won't think much of you. As a result, they will treat you less than you deserve.

If they really love you and love themselves, then they will know how to treat you in the process. Their actions will show you, better than their words can tell you. Their actions will let you know, if it's real love or lip service. Real love is expressed in how they treat you, not just what they say to you. Indeed love is a verb, it requires action. Don't just say it, show it!

Don't believe what they say, at the expense of ignoring what you see. Love is action and it will show through, in how someone treats you. Words fall on deaf ears, when actions are seen with wide eyes. Real love doesn't tear you down. It lifts you up. When it's real love, you won't have to question it. The answers will show in their actions. The right one will recognize your value. They can clearly see, that you are a red box and a gold bow. You're a gift to the world. If people don't recognize your value, that's their loss. Never lose sight of the gift and value that God placed within you. If you're single, divorced, separated, or married you must know your value whether or not someone is with you.

Don't let someone's mismanagement of love, stop you from believing in love. Don't allow disappointments to stop you from expecting to receive love. The right person will make you realize, why the wrong one never worked in the first place. Discernment will show you the difference, between the right one and the one right now. Don't get in such a hurry, that you settle for less than God's intended best for your life. If you get in God's way, you will shake your head and say, "Why did I get married?" The one that's right for you, is more important than the rush to say "I do."

CHAPTER 5

Beautiful Scars

God will heal your scars and bring beauty out of your pain.

When you take a glance into the mirror of your soul, you will recognize that the ugly situations you went through brought out the beauty in you. No, it didn't feel good to you, but it unlocked something greater in you. You've heard the statement, "We don't always realize how strong we are, until being strong is our only option." I'd like to convey, we don't always realize how handsome or beautiful we are, until we press through some ugly situations. You are not what happened to you. Neither are you the mistakes that you've made. Don't let what's behind you define you, when the best of you is ahead for you.

WISDOM FROM WOUNDS

I burned my finger a short time ago, while cooking. Don't laugh, I really am a good cook. I've got some chef skills. So, I soaked my finger in cold water to cool off the burn. I even applied some cocoa butter to it. Over the next few days, the burn seemingly got worse and uglier before it got better. So to make it more appealing to the eye, I started to peel the skin. I began to realize that my finger couldn't heal properly, until I stopped picking at the wound.

I convey this example to you, because sometimes a setback, heartache, and heartbreak burns the very fiber of our being. We think we're cooking with someone who is good looking. All of a sudden, things go in the opposite direction of what we expected and now we're wounded. Consequently, we pick at our hurt, wounds, and rejection. We pick apart our own lives, as a result of the scars that caused us pain. Sometimes things get worse before they get better. However, you have to refuse to be bitter. You won't heal, if you keep picking at what and who wounded you. I know they should be held accountable for hurting you, but you have to be responsible for the healing within you. Allow God to bring healing to you. Yes, you may have the scar, but God will heal you of the pain. Realize your beauty is not only in your smile. It's also in your scars. God will give you beauty from brokenness and wisdom from your wounds.

YOU ARE ENOUGH

In a superficial world, being attractive and beautiful is measured by societal standards. Are you tall enough, small enough, dark or light enough? Not much long enough, you start asking yourself the question, "Are you enough?" I know you've been through some tough stuff, but don't fail to realize you are enough. You know you're blessed, when you don't look like what you've been through. God brought you through. What you endured didn't reduce you, it produced greater strength within you. Love you. Celebrate you. Value you and the right people will too. You're too unique to compete and too rare to compare. Love isn't competition. It's collaboration and devotion. Yes, your royalty demands loyalty, but you first have to recognize it within yourself. You are a royal priesthood, according to I Peter 2:9. Wear your crown. Be loyal to the royal greatness that God placed within you. Speak life over your life and tell yourself, "I am enough!" You will always feel incomplete, when you try to compete. Realize you're divinely designed with a purpose in mind. You're special just the way you are. Love the skin you're in. Look within and recognize your value within!

BEAUTY FOR ASHES

I'm reminded of a true story, about a woman named Naomi Oni from London. Much of her story has come to light, as she has gained courage to share her painful experience. In December of 2012 on a routine day, Naomi ventured home via the transit station. She recalls getting off the bus, en route home and noticed someone in a veiled garment following her. She remembered the cold stare, they gave her as she turned to look back. Naomi crossed the street, being only a few minutes from her house and noticed the stranger continued to follow her. As Naomi turned her head, all of a sudden she felt a splash of liquid on her face. Namoi ran home, as the acid began to eat away at her scalp and skin. How could such a gruesome and vile attack, happen to such a beautiful person? Why did this happen to her? These were the questions that Naomi asked herself repeatedly.

I wonder have you ever been in a terrible situation, where you realized you've been a pretty good person. You go to church, pay your tithes and offering, mentor, assist in the community, and help others in need. As a result you say, "Why is this happening to me?" You could literally think of about ten different people, who should be in the situation that you find yourself in. I know that I asked that same question as a teenager, grappling to live when I was diagnosed with stage four cancer. I was just starting my life and I found myself fighting, not to lose my life. Like Naomi, I was unaware that the attack of affliction was coming. What do you do, when the beautiful life you dreamed of becomes a daunting and ugly nightmare?

As I was fighting, I never received my healing until I stopped complaining. I had to believe, as hard as I prayed. I had to stop blaming others, for the circumstance that I found myself in. I had to realize that this battle was not mine, but it belongs to the Lord. Yes, cancer made me cry, but it didn't make me quit. It bruised me, but it didn't beat me. It scarred me, but God healed me. I found the CAN in cancer.

What do you do, when the perpetrator is familiar to you? Little did Naomi know, that someone she called a "friend" was behind the veil. They followed her and eventually threw acid on her face. The female "friend" even texted Naomi, to see if she was okay and had the nerve to show up to her birthday party. I'm still in awe, at the evil wolf in sheep's clothing mentality. I mean with friends like that, who needs enemies? The perpetrator was eventually apprehended and imprisoned, but the time served cannot erase the scars inflicted.

Naomi had to endure a process of forgiveness and healing, that was not only on the outside but from the inside. She conveyed the fact that the attack, had a tremendous impact on her life. Even more so, due to being betrayed by a "friend." Naomi battled with thoughts of suicide and couldn't bear to look at herself in the mirror. The scarring from the acid disfigured her face, neck, and chest. The tears Naomi shed, could fill a river bank. She remembers saying to herself, "Who will want to marry me like this?" Thankfully God blessed her with a relationship, where her man saw the beauty in her scars.

The power of forgiveness, freed Naomi from the pain

of bitterness. She decided to forgive the "friend" who was jealous and committed the heinous act. Despite your weeping, know that joy is coming. The tears you've sown, are watering the seeds of strength for your harvest. Even in your place of discontent and grief, God will give you "Beauty for ashes, the oil of joy for mourning, and the garment of praise for the spirit of heaviness" (Isaiah 61:3). God will get greater glory from your story. Your seeming tragedy, will become a triumphant journey and testimony.

SCARS TO STARS

So often what people have dumped on us, has become our lot and lifestyle. They have dumped abuse, hurt, pain, shame, manipulation, rejection, animosity, and bitterness on our lives. We now internalize what they have done to us and turn on ourselves as a result. We begin to think something is wrong with us and no one will love us, because of the scars that we now wear. Realize that it's not over for you.

Much like Naomi, people burned you, but God still preserved you. They afflicted you, but God still blessed and gifted you. The fight is fixed and you will win in the end. Something beautiful is coming out of you, despite what you've been through. The right one for you is committed to love you, despite the scars that life has inflicted on you.

A person is not only handsome or beautiful, based upon how they look on the outside. It originates with who they are on the inside. Don't become ugly, because you were treated ugly. There is something beautiful, coming out of your scars. God will transform your scars into stars. The light in you, will outshine the darkness that surrounds you. God will bring you out of darkness, into the magnanimity of His marvelous light. Yes, you've got some scars, but animosity, envy, and jealousy can't destroy your beauty and destiny. What happens when everything in life, is stripped away and all we're left with is our scars from yesterday? Money can't buy it, surgery can't repair it, a meal can't fill it, clothes or makeup can't cover it. Only God's power, can release you and help you to recover from it.

LESSONS AND BLESSINGS

Take comfort in knowing, that God will place people in your life, that see you beyond the scars that you've been through. The right one will see the value in you, rather than focus on the circumstances you've been through. They will see the best in you and want the best for you. They won't inflict the pain of your past on you. The right one won't use your mistakes against you, as a power struggle to manipulate you. They see your heart, not just your hurt. They see the power of your future, despite the pain of your past. The worst thing that someone can do, is to put you through the pain of what you've already been through. You've had enough bruises and scars. You've grappled with enough bad decisions, now God is providing Good Samaritans. They will bless you, bandage your wounds, and assist in your breakthrough. They won't ask, "What will I lose by helping you?" They will focus on what you will gain, because God called them to bless you. Let go of the bitterness and strife that erodes your life. See the value in your experiences. Don't discount yourself. Know your worth. The lessons will become greater blessings.

BEAUTY IS ONLY SKIN DEEP

I'm sure you've heard the statement, "It hurts to look beautiful." It's conveyed from the aspect, that enduring pain births pristine beauty despite one's suffering. More than hurting to look beautiful, it hurts even more to live as a victim of your ugly past and not blossom into something beautiful. Yes, beauty comes in all shapes and sizes, but it also comes in all strengths and struggles. The beautiful part of life is not always the rose. Sometimes it's the thorns. It's not always the makeup or mascara. Sometimes it's revealed by taking off the mask. It's not always the suit. Sometimes it's the scars underneath. It's not always in the breakthrough. Sometimes it's in the betrayal, that didn't break you. It's in the blessing of being able to go through and not look like, what you've been through. Beauty is only skin deep, but from your scars and soul, the depth of who you are speaks. Will you communicate from your purpose or from your pain? Despite the scars on and in you, God is bringing beauty out of you. More than natural but emotional, mental, and spiritual enhancements. If beauty doesn't come from within, you will always be without it.

If someone tells you that the dress you're wearing is beautiful, it's really not a compliment. The dress was beautiful on a mannequin or on the retail rack. However, if they tell you that you're beautiful, now that's a compliment. You can complement their life. At the end of the day, it's not about what you have on you. It's about the value that resides within you, which makes you beautiful. Your beauty must not only reside in you physically. It must be rooted emotionally, mentally, and spiritually.

Realize the ugly things you went through, unveiled the beauty in you. God is the author. You're getting ready to flip the page and write a new chapter. You're too beautiful, to stay in situations that make you feel ugly. See the beauty in you. God will heal the scars that afflicted you. This time the tears that flow, will be an expression of joy. At last, you're released from the past. Don't give up, get up and try it again. Despite your scars my friend, God is about to make your life beautiful again!

CHAPTER 6

Wife for Life

You are the kind of wife, who will improve a man's life.

The term "wife" is more than a title, it's a function. It's the life you live. It's the way that you prepare yourself now, for what is to come. A ring doesn't mean anything, if the right man from God, doesn't put it on your finger. More than carats, a wife of noble character is focused on a man's character. Beyond what he drives, discover what's driving him. More than what's in his wallet, does he have wisdom? After you admire his designer glasses, what is his vision? You see, what's built on sand can't stand. Yes, the right amount of money can attain what's superficial. However, you can't put a price on what's faithful with a foundation that's spiritual.

Realize that you can't make a man love you or marry you. Sis, you can't change a man. The best thing you can do, is to pray for him. If God doesn't change him, then he doesn't want to be changed. If God removes him, don't try to rescue him. Let it go, better is coming. The right one will recognize your value. It's not your job to twist someone's arm, to make them see in you, what they choose to remain blind to. If they don't see it, they weren't given the eyes for it. Please understand, it's not worth keeping them at the expense of losing you. If they don't see your worth, they're not worth your time.

Don't lose your mind over the relationship that was lost. You're going to need your mind, for the marriage that's coming. Don't lose your mind over what scarred you, because you're going to need your mind, for the right man to embrace the beauty in you. Don't go back and get what God delivered you from. Why settle for someone who is a perpetrator, abuser, and a liar? You don't have time for drama and dream killers. The right man has eyes to recognize, you are a **WIFE** who is *Wisely Inspired Faithfully Empowered.*

WOMAN OF WORTH

You're a woman of worth. There is a queen in you and your royalty demands loyalty. The right one for you, knows that a woman like you is in rare air and the answer to the right man's prayer. A king can't find a queen like you anywhere. See the beauty in you and celebrate the gift, that God put in you. A rare woman like you is the kind of wife, that will add value to a man's life. What God is preparing, is worth you waiting. Let God work on you, for what He's prepared for you. Don't rush fast, into what you want to last. It's worth it, to wait on it. Stop stressing over it or settling, just to say you have somebody. It's better to wait long, than to settle for a relationship that's not worth it at all. As you've been praying and waiting, God will release your blessing.

VISION FOR PROVISION

For all of the times you've wondered why, God was always making a way. Don't get in His way. Keep pressing toward your vision to receive provision. The right person, the right opportunity, and the right blessing is coming. It's worth you waiting for it. Open your eyes to see it, so you can receive it. Love yourself, walk in your purpose, and keep making progress. It's worth the wait, to receive the best and blessed!

SUCCESSFULLY SINGLE

A few years ago, I spoke at a Women's Empowerment Expo. I was also included with a few other gentlemen, for the "Black Men Revealed" panel. I along with the panelists, shared insight with more than 1,000 women about love, relationships, and what men want. During the Q&A session, the moderator asked each of us, "Why are you single?" One gentleman explained, that he was focused on his business pursuits. Another man affirmed, he was taking his time until it's the right time. Then it was my turn. As all eyes were on me, I conveyed the fact that I'm preparing my life for my wife spiritually, financially, physically, and emotionally. I only intend to marry one time and make it last forever. So in my season of singleness, I'm being selective. My daily walk is in preparedness and wholeness. Being successful in my singleness, is a blueprint for a marriage of peace and purpose. I know that God is preparing me, to be a holistic husband to the woman that He's prepared for me. As I'm working, preparing, and praying, God will lead me to find the woman that He has for me.

HE'S PRAYING FOR YOU

The right man is faithfully praying to God, that he gets to marry a woman like you. Just like you are saving yourself for him, know that he is also saving himself for you. The same purity that he wants from you, is what he's pursuing too. He exercises self-discipline. He pursues his purpose. He diligently works his job and builds his business. He is developing himself intellectually and interpersonally. He is maturing spiritually and letting God lead him daily.

The right man for you, is preparing for a life with you. He recognizes that his presence is a present. So, he doesn't share his time with just any and everyone. He knows that a woman like you, is rare and the answer to the right man's prayer. He knows you're worth the wait, because you're the kind of wife that will add value to his life. The right man is praying for a woman like you and working on himself, to be a good husband to you. Don't rush it. Trust it and rest knowing it. A precious jewel like you, will be loved by the man that God has for you.

Stay ready it's coming. As sure as you're reading, it's closer than you're thinking. More than what you can imagine, it will happen. Beyond just a wedding, your marriage will be a blessing. God is connecting you both, as purpose partners for each other. Prepare yourself to say, "I do" to the right man who is praying and has a plan to marry you!

ARE YOU READY?

When you meet the right man, you won't have time to get ready. You will need to already be ready. Like they say, "If you stay ready, you won't have to get ready." God has what you want. It's ready for you, but are you ready for it?

When everyone is going to happy hour, get happy and go to the gym for an hour. While everyone else is clubbing, learn how to perfect your cooking. When everyone is going out, will you stay in and build your business? When all of the rest are surrounding themselves with any and everybody, will you value your body?

Far too often, we have made marriage an idol. As a result we remain idle. You say you're waiting on God, when He's waiting on you to fulfill the vision He gave you. Can God trust you to do what He told you, before a man marries you? Might your obedience be the requirement, that unlocks the door to your happily ever after? I Corinthians 7:34 declares, "The unmarried woman careth for the things of the Lord, that she may be holy both in body and in spirit." In your singleness, allow God to bring purity and wholeness to you mentally, physically, and spiritually.

FINE WITH FAVOR

Let God give you the right man, who has a heart to love you and grow with you. Proverbs 18:22 declares, "He who finds a wife, finds a good thing and obtains favor from the Lord." Anything that's worth finding, is not easy to find. You're fine, but you also have favor. Are you that "good thing" that's worth finding?

Your love is worth waiting for and looking for. You are the favor that a man receives for his labor. You don't just become a wife, when you get married and march down the aisle to say your vows. The Bible calls you a "wife" before a man finds you and marries you. Essentially, when you align yourself spiritually and interpersonally to develop, you adopt the qualities of a wife. However, when the right man marries you, then you become his wife. Your skills, talents, abilities, and favor will improve his life. The fruitful essence of your femininity, royalty, and identity brings a man stability.

TRUST IT, DON'T RUSH IT

Don't try to rush or fit, what doesn't belong in your life. You will ruin it, if you rush it. Take the time to pause, pray, and be patient. Let God direct you to it, so you don't waste time rushing it. Sometimes we're in a hurry, going nowhere. Pausing, praying, and waiting does not mean you're wasting time. Keep preparing, working, and trusting. What you're expecting is coming. Let God reveal to you, who is good for you. What you would choose, doesn't compare to the best choice that He has for you. When the right man has you, he will thank God for blessing him with a woman like you.

Everything comes to you in the right moment, so be patient.

Your patience is preparing you for your promise. All of the moments of hurt, trials, isolation, rejection, and pain won't compare to your moment of joy. Everything you've hoped for, is worth you waiting for. Expect to receive more. I've learned, when you move out of the way then God will create a way. Don't rush it. Be patient as you expect it. God will do it. The financial breakthrough, business, promotion, marriage, and blessing is coming to you. Keep working the vision within you. More than just anything or something, God is about to give you everything. It will be more than what you're expecting.

Just as you're reading it, God is arranging it. He is preparing you, for who He has for you. Don't chase it, trust it. Don't force it, but have the faith for it. Your purpose partner is not delayed or denied. It will happen at the right time. Develop the love within, before you seek it from them. As you're preparing for your spouse, make sure order is in your house. God is going to do it and connect it, quicker than you expect it.

PREPARE FOR WHAT'S PREPARED

God has already prepared the way for you. So know that He is just preparing you. In essence, God is preparing you for what He's prepared for you. Trust Him with every step you take. You're getting ready to accelerate and elevate. It's not delayed or denied. Be encouraged in knowing, that the right things will happen for you at the right time. Get out of your own way. God has prepared the way. Stay positioned and prepared, so you can step into what God has prepared. Everything is aligning for you, even the right one that God has for you. Remain in alignment with God's divine assignment!

You're too unique to compete and too rare to compare. You're too valuable to settle, for anything less than God's best. As you pursue your purpose, the right things and person will pursue you. Know that you're chosen to receive it. Everything you've been through prepared you, for where God is taking you. The disappointments, dismay, depression, and dark days will become your testimony, to triumph over adversity. Every prayer you've prayed and every tear you've cried, prepared you. Get ready to receive what God has for you.

PAUSE AND PRAISE

Take a moment to stop and thank God, for how far He brought you. It prepared you for where He's taking you. Yes, you've had more victories than losses. More blessings than lessons. Focus on your strengths not your struggles. What you've been striving to do, will now pay off for you. Better is coming, as a result of what you've been through. Your prayers, tears, effort, and selflessness doesn't go unnoticed. All along, God was counting every prayer, tear, and will restore your years. Don't give up. Your blessing is near. You owe it to you, to look within and see the beauty in you. Count your blessings not your burdens. Pause and praise God, not just for where you're going or where you've been. Pause and praise Him, for what He placed within to help you win.

TAKE A SELFIE SISTER

You owe it to you, to see the beauty and blessing that is you. Before you expect a man to see your value, do you see your own? Count your miracles not your missteps. For all of the times you've screamed silently, get ready to shout in victory. Do yourself a favor. The next time you take a selfie, don't just look at it. Look through it. Look through the core, to see all of the blessings God has in store. Look through the mirror of your soul, to see your essence and substance. See the grace and greatness within you. Look past the makeup, to see the miracle. Beyond the red lipstick, see real love. Beyond your hairdo, see the new and improved you. See more than your heels. Look to the hills because your help

comes from the Lord. The next time you take a selfie, don't

just admire your curvaceous body. Celebrate your inner

beauty.

GOD'S PLAN

Just like you're worth the wait, so is a Godly relationship.

Understand, it may not be your time to date. It just might be

your time to wait. In the meantime, let God work on you for

what He's prepared for you. Don't rush fast, into what you

want to last. The pain of an ex, won't compare to the

blessing that's coming next. Your future will be brighter than

your past. Take comfort in knowing, what God promised

will come to pass. It's worth it, to wait on it. Don't interrupt

God's plan, because things aren't happening according to

your plan. Stop stressing over it or settling, just to say you

have somebody. It's better to wait long, than to settle for a

relationship that's not worth it at all. Let God bring

wholeness in your season of singleness. Love yourself, walk in your purpose, and keep making progress. Prepare yourself to be the best and receive the best.

If God wants you to be with someone, trust Him to make it happen at the right time and with the right one. Never make permanent decisions with temporary feelings. The right one will bring rest, not stress. Don't force someone to be, where they don't have the desire to stay. Remain aligned, so you can receive what God has assigned. He is sending the right one. Be patient this time. It will happen at the right time.

UNWRAP THE GIFT IN YOU

What good is it to receive a beautifully wrapped box, only to open it and see nothing inside? You would be disappointed because the inside, was void of the projected value on the outside. Could someone see the beauty of you, if they had no sight? Beauty will attract a man, but it won't keep a man. Of the makings of beautiful women, there is no end.

Yes, you're fine but what else? What is it to have a body, but not a mind? The real gift of you, goes beyond the physical beauty that preoccupies you. Do you recognize your gift within? Are you using it, to bring glory to Him? Oftentimes, we are so focused on the outside, that we rarely take the time to nurture the treasure on the inside. Yes, your outer frame will attract him to you. However your peace, presence, perspective, and personality will keep him with you. Too often we hear the disparaging statement, "No man can be faithful." However, the right one that God has for you, is well equipped and able. Change what you're thinking and confessing. As a result, you will change what you're attracting. Can you speak to the king in a man? Can you encourage and pray him through, what he goes through?

RING THE ALARM

Are you peaceful or vengeful? Well you say, "I'll put a man in his place if I have to." Will putting him in his place, cause you to lose your place? A man is not a project, for you to break down and build up. It's not your job to chase and chastise him. You will drive yourself crazy. Instead of being his pressure, can you be his place of peace? A man doesn't want to have to fight in the ring and in the corner too. A boxer expects to get hit in the ring, but not in the corner. The bell rings per round, so a boxer can go in their corner and get treated for the hits they incur. When a man has suffered the lacerations of life, will you further hit him or stop the bleeding? Will you inflict pain or infuse peace in his presence?

WAKANDA WOMAN ARE YOU?

I must confess, I am not much of a movie buff. I very rarely take the time, to check out the hottest cinema screenings.

However, I did watch the movie *Black Panther* a time or two. The movie was a cultural phenomenon. Not only did it show the beauty of African people, but it debunked the negative propaganda that only European culture is advanced. Although millions of people saw the movie, many didn't see it because they missed the mind-blowing moments in it.

Generally, when you see black women depicted in mass media, it is often from a disparaging point of view. They are depicted as loud, rude, crude, and crass. Either fighting over a man or fighting each other, for the attention of a man. This indeed is a stereotype. However, the movie *Black Panther* provided a prototype. In the film, women were protecting one another and fighting for each other, rather than over a man or against one another.

Real queens don't compete, they collaborate. They don't chase a man. They chase their purpose and plan. They are too unique to compete and too rare to compare. As a result, they wear their crown and build their queendom in the kingdom of God. So the question becomes "Wakanda" woman are you?

The women who lived in the fictional country of Wakanda, had four prominent characteristics that are significant to adopt. They were warriors, direction driven discerners, healers, and purpose partners.

In the film, the women of Wakanda were warriors. It's a true depiction, that black women have always defended black men. Too often women stand on the frontline, when we as men stand on the sidelines. No, you don't have a spear, but you do have spirit. The best warrior that you can be, is a prayer warrior. Don't be a worrier. You're a fighter who is a warrior. God gave you the victory, despite all of the public and secret battles that you've faced. You fought with your tears, your mentality, and your praise. God went to battle for you. Realize that you don't need a superpower. Your prayer life, relationship with God, determination, intelligence, and inner strength is your superpower.

The women of Wakanda exemplified direction driven discernment. They could sense imminent danger and avoid detours to destruction. There is a quote that suggests, "No nation can rise higher than its women." The reason you have risen, is because you have discernment and direction. God is ordering your steps, to inform you of what to avoid and the paths to take. Your prayer life is the compass, that will direct you into your destiny. God's direction is for your protection.

As healers, King T'Challa's mother and sister brought him back to life, after he fought to the death. To the brother who is reading, despite your dream that may be dead or on life support, the healing hands and prayers of a woman will bring it back to life. Psalm 46:5 declares, "God is within her, she will not fail." As a woman, sometimes you find yourself leading while bleeding. Helping everyone else while you're hurting. Ultimately hurting people, hurt people but healed people will heal people. You can't truly bring healing into the lives of others, until you let God heal you from within. When you do, then whatever you put your hands to will prosper.

Lastly, the women of Wakanda were purpose partners. It's worth noting, that they couldn't help a man who didn't have a purpose. Sis, it's not your job to raise a man or treat him like a build-a-bear. Don't raise him, release him. Let God put the man together and present him to you. A purpose partner will bring something to the table, so you both can collaborate. At the end of the day, I can't help you if you can't help you. More than having a queen, the king needed a woman warrior and most importantly a purpose partner.

EYES FOR YOU

Don't let anyone make you feel, that your desire is too big for God to fulfill. Know that you are the kind of wife, who will improve a man's life. There is never a shortage of purpose partners, when God is the supplier. He will "Supply all of your need, according to His riches in glory by Christ

Jesus" (Philippians 4:19). Realize that you're about to go from overlooked, to married and took. The right one, won't be blind to the blessing of you. They see the value in you. Don't complain, compete, or compare. God has something special for you, because you're rare. What He is preparing, is worth you waiting. Don't rush it, God is doing it. Settling is not worth it, just to appease everybody. It's never the right time, if it's the wrong person who doesn't fit your purpose.

The wrong one overlooked you, because the right one only has eyes for you. The times you've cried, the patience you've shown, the prayers you've prayed, and the years you've prepared were all developing you for the spouse God has for you. Let them drag their feet if they want to. The next time they look, you will be married and took. Even when they were overlooking you, God was always looking over you. All along, He was preparing you for who and what He has for you.

To the world you are just one person, but to the right

person you will be their world. They will only have eyes for you, to see in you what everyone else was blind to. God has the right someone for you. Realize that your "someday" is soon to come any day. God has the whole world in His hands, so allow Him to place your love in the right hands. Whether locally or globally, God has the right one for you uniquely. They won't just look at what's on you. They will see the love, purpose, strength, vision, and value in you. Don't rush it or doubt it. God is orchestrating it. You will be the right man's wife for life. When the right one looks at you, they will thank God for giving them the best person in the world, which is YOU!

CHAPTER 7

Genesis of a Gentleman

A gentleman respects a lady, manages his time wisely, and manifests his destiny.

C ontrary to popular belief, chivalry is not dead. It just seems to be on life support. When did opening doors, giving a woman flowers, respect, and being a gentleman stop being the norm? When did a quality of strength, become that which is deemed to be soft? Misogyny and chauvinism, seems to outshine chivalry these days. Let's make being husbands, scholars, fathers, leaders, mentors, and gentleman great again.

A gentleman is one who personifies strength and gentleness in his character. The genesis of a gentleman emanates from his connection to God, an understanding of

WIFE - Dr. Eddie Connor

self, and the value that he brings to a relationship. Kind acts of chivalry, communication, respecting, and treating a woman like a queen is rooted in his character. He seeks to protect a woman's heart and love her to life. What does this mean to a brother, who has lacked love throughout his life? It wasn't present in the home, community, relationships, and much less in his own life. As men we know how to be tough, but who will teach us to be gentle? Generally our view of being gentle is seen as delicate, fragile, weak, soft, and yes feminine. A skewed view of masculinity only perpetuates toughness, a lack of emotion, and competition. Being polite doesn't make you a punk. Exhibiting strength to love, doesn't make you soft.

GROWN AND GROWING

Growing up, I thought all of those aforementioned qualities were equivalent to being soft. My trust diminished and obstinate attitude increased, after my parents' divorce. My father was absent, throughout the adolescent years of my life which scarred me. I internalized that pain and shifted into "tough guy" mode. At least I thought I was tough. I got into my fair share of fights, because I was angry and didn't address the root cause of my attitude. Yes, my loving mother was there for me, but she wasn't my father. The man I look like, didn't come to my basketball games. He didn't talk to me about girls, show me how to shave my beard, or share the intangible elements of what it meant to be a man, much less a gentleman. He never affirmed the boy or man in me.

I'm grateful though for the men, who have mentored me and planted seeds of strength in my life. I've seen them loving their wives, building businesses, making an honest living, mentoring in the community, rehabilitating their life, and making indelible marks that can never be erased. I am the man, I am today because of them. I am also the man, I am today because of what I didn't have. It made me stronger, wiser, resilient, and a gentleman. My grandfather was such a tremendous influence, to develop me in my formative years. Even in death, his life shaped the course of my life. He was a devoted husband, father, teacher, civil rights advocate, mentor, athlete, musician, deacon, decorated World War II Veteran, and gentleman. The only father figure I had, who taught me how to tie-a-tie as a boy. He gave me invaluable wisdom as a man. I would walk through his home and hear him singing, "If I can help somebody as I pass along, then my living will not be in vain." He was not only successful but significant. He helped so many people during his journey. I'm sincerely striving to leave a lasting legacy, just like my grandfather.

One of his most awe inspiring traits, was how gentle he was with my grandmother. He wasn't weak, soft, or docile. He was strong and constrained that strength with tender loving care. He was the quintessential gentleman, who was always well-dressed. His nickname for my grandmother was "Angel." He called her "Angel" so much, that I thought it was her real name. He believed that my grandmother, was the angel that God sent him. What my father did not do for me, God sent other men and my grandfather to pour into me.

As I grew older, I was at a crossroads to remain a grown boy or decide to man up and take responsibility for my life. I decided the latter. I would have missed the blessings in the lessons, if I remained bitter. When I made a conscientious decision to forgive my father, then I was truly able to live. No, I don't have it all together. I'm not perfect, but each day by God's grace, I'm striving to be better. Yes, I'm grown, but I'm challenging myself to keep growing.

MAN UP: BOYS TO MEN

In this generation, we are seeing an ever increasing number of grown boys. Yes, grown boys at 20, 30, 40, 50+ years of age. Many are void of maturity and responsibility. If you only look like what you are void of, then you are a wolf in sheep's clothing. Sadly our women and children, have become victims at the hands of grown boys, who prey on their vulnerability. A gentleman will protect and pray for you, but only grown boys will play and prey on you.

The soulful Blues singer, Muddy Waters would have referred to a "grown boy" today as a "man child." In 1955, during a time of segregation and Jim Crow, Waters released a song, *Mannish Boy*. If you listen to the song, you can hear Waters soulfully crooning and vociferously declaring himself to be "a man." He did this at a time, when black men were often referred to as "boys." Many black men were demonized and dehumanized, in an era of inequality. Muddy Waters, the Father of Chicago Blues, stepped into murky waters. As a musician, Muddy used every growl in his voice and guitar riff. It seemed to free him from systemic racism and societal oppression. He sang and proclaimed, "I'm a man, m-a-n."

To juxtapose the narrative, Waters ebulliently celebrated his boyish ways of being "a man child" and a rolling stone. Symbolically, these terms are ailments in our society today. True manhood must be immersed, in a cohesion of declaration and demonstration via our daily actions.

To only possess style and sensuality, precludes you from walking in true manhood and masculinity. Growth that only happens physically, but lacks mentally and spiritually is immaturity. Our boys will never develop into men, until we free them from a "grown boy" mentality. We must teach them to be gentlemen. To be a full-grown man is to transition from the shadows of boyhood, into the sunlit path, as a gentleman via brotherhood and manhood.

A gentleman respects a lady, manages his time wisely, and manifests his destiny. He provides for his family and protects his community. The true test of what it means to be a man, is found in I Corinthians 13:11. The scripture declares, "When I was a child, I spake as a child, I understood as a child, I thought as a child: but when I became a man, I put away childish things." What are you willing to put away, in order to become? What are you willing to leave behind, in order to move ahead? What will you give up, in order to discover and gain true growth? This is the true test of manhood.

SIZE MATTERS

The true measure of a gentleman, is what he is willing to let go of to gain. In a hypersexualized culture, we are inundated with images that speak to virility and pseudomasculinity, but not spirituality and sagacity. As a result, men become well-equipped to make love, but heartless when it comes to expressing love. Being a man is not about what's in your pants or your pocket. It's about what's in your head and your heart. What we possess below the waist, doesn't equate to the strength above our neck. The power of our spirit and mind, can push us forward to redeem the time. The size of our inner strength and sacrifice, speaks to the true measure of a man.

Will you measure up to your responsibility? What is the size and strength of your love? Are you willing to go the extra mile? Where your energy goes, commitment flows. A gentleman is not driven by ego, but purpose driven to discover how he can grow. Purpose must be the engine, that propels us on the road to our destination. Mythical masculinity and machismo, is never greater than maturity.

THE MASK OF MASCULINITY

The impediments of our culture have produced a powder keg of emotionless, communicatively deficient, and narcissistic males in today's generation. Sadly there is a generation of misogynistic grown boys, masquerading as men, but only operating as insecure males. They exist with a false sense of bravado and mythical masculinity, which is only a shield to mask the hurt, pain, and vulnerability. The smoky mirror of masculinity, contains more shadow than substance.

Scripture warned us, "In the last days perilous times shall come. For men shall be lovers of themselves, covetous, boasters, proud, blasphemers, disobedient to parents, unthankful, unholy, without natural affection, trucebreakers, false accusers, incontinent, fierce, despisers of those that are good, traitors, heady, high-minded, and lovers of pleasures more than lovers of God" (II Timothy 3:1-4). We are seeing this current epidemic, become a cultural pandemic, adversely affecting the lives of our brothers.

LOVE IN ACTION

How can we say that we love our sisters, if we disrespect them? A true gentleman and king, will treat a woman like a queen. Even if she doesn't see herself as one. Why harbor hatred against your brother? When you truly love yourself, you will express love to your brothers and sisters. We have so many brothers and sisters who are angry, but don't even know why. They're hurting and can't even express the pain, that they're feeling. They have become so numb to pain, that it now hurts to be happy. They mask the pain with drugs, alcohol, sex, violence, and self-destructive behaviors, that never remedy the root of their issues.

Far too often, our brothers have been dropped in the home and in society. Who will pick them up? The hands that were supposed to heal and help them, only brought hurt and harm to their lives. We often hear the statistic, 1 in 3 girls are sexually abused. We must also note, 1 in 6 boys are sexually abused before age 18. Rather than speak up about it, we tuck the pain away and act out of rage. Never getting the therapy, clarity, or ridding ourselves of the anger and animosity. We have not created a culture for men, to be open about their hurts, flaws, and weaknesses. We have shunned and shelved it as femininity, sensitivity, and made no concession for vulnerability. If we allow our boys to be destroyed, they will never become the men that they are destined to be. We will either build strong boys or repair broken men.

The mythical masculine culture framed it, that even when you fell off a bike as a child, you were told to "Stand up and stop crying." As a boy they said to you, "Be a man." How can you be a man, in your developmental years when you're just a child? It takes growth, maturity, and time. Our toughness must never be called into question, because we cried. It should be answered by wiping our tears, healing, and pushing ahead, despite the pain. Now, when males reach the age where they should be a man, we are seeing them choose to rebel and behave like boys.

BROTHER FROM ANOTHER MOTHER

Who do we talk to, when we are dealing with issues?

Honestly, there are certain things that we can't talk to our sisters about. Sometimes we need another brother to confide in. Who do you turn to, if everyone is "acting tough" and refusing to acknowledge their weaknesses? Can we turn to our brothers and seek help, or are we too busy competing with each other and isolating ourselves in caves of calamity? True brotherhood goes beyond blood. It's forged by a bond. In good and bad times, a real brother empowers you through circumstances because we all need second chances. Proverbs 17:17 declares, "A brother is born for adversity." Not to cause it, but to help you overcome it.

Competition is for the basketball court, not the beloved community. We must start building each other and stop competing against each other. We know how to be smooth and debonair. We know how to act tough. We know how to put up our guard and cloak ourselves, in a false sense of bravado. We know how to act like we have it all together. We have learned those steps, like a dance routine. However, do we know how to provide, protect, and empower one another? Do we know how to be gentlemen? Do we know how to truly be our brother's keeper and sister's protector?

SUPERMAN SYNDROME

As brothers we must confess, the "S" on our chest doesn't always stand for Superman, success, or strength. Sometimes the "S" on our chest, symbolizes that we're struggling. Many times we struggle with insecurity, identity, feeling incomplete, addiction, and fatherlessness. We have been taught to repress our feelings, rather than to express them. So, for years we harbor feelings of abandonment, societal trials, the ravages of racism, searching for purpose, and the reality of what it takes to be a man.

CLARK KENT

We must take off the mask to uncover the machismo, muscles, and money to peer into our vulnerability. When we do, we will understand that we're more like Clark Kent than

Superman. Our flashes of greatness, have been forged through the fire of grit and grief. The essence of manpower, is not in what you possess. It's in understanding your purpose. It's not in what you have. It's in who you are.

You can never know WHO you are, until you understand WHOSE you are. When you develop your relationship with God (your spiritual father), then you will exercise your purpose and power from within. True manpower unlocks the door of destiny and serves to guide others to greatness.

NICE FOR WHAT

It's so easy for us as men and women to be savages, due to how we have been hurt and damaged. If we don't take the time to heal and walk in wholeness, we will perpetuate that same negativity toward one another. In our rage, anger, and impulsiveness we have damaged women's hearts. Some women have insulated and isolated themselves, to where they have now become "the men" that they expected us to be. Their strength and resilience, has seemingly out muscled ours.

So, what would I be nice for, when my kindness is taken for weakness? The strength to stand firm, is not contingent upon how people perceive it. The power is in how you choose to act upon it, by believing it. Healing, joy, wholeness, standards, purity, peace, love, and responsibility is not only for women. It's for us as men too. Sis, just because a man is nice, doesn't mean he's void of a backbone. Niceness is not a cloak for weakness. Chivalry doesn't make us a chump. Being gentle isn't reserved for women. It's essence is rooted in true manhood, masculinity, identity, strength, and responsibility.

REAL GENTLEMEN

Being a gentleman is about how you treat and respect yourself, before you step into the presence of a woman. If you don't respect you, then you will never respect her too.

Being a gentleman, is about more than wearing a Brioni suit

and a Zegna tie. Are you clothed in strength and tied to

becoming a better man? It's about more than the Ferragamo

shoes on your feet. It's about allowing God to order your

steps, so you can lead those who follow you. Being a

gentleman, is not about the Rolex watch on your wrist. It's

about recognizing that it's time to man up. It's more than

wearing Clive Christian cologne. It's about being a Christian

with your actions, mind, and soul. Real gentlemen raise their

mentality, manifest their destiny, and manage their gifts with

urgency. No, chivalry is not dead, because a real gentleman

keeps it alive. Holding doors, holding hands, and holding a

woman's heart with tender loving care is in our DNA.

GENTLEMAN'S GUIDE TO GREATNESS

Gentlemen are honest.
Gentlemen are intelligent.
Gentlemen build their community and bring unity.
Gentlemen are confident not arrogant.

W I F E - DR. EDDIE CONNOR

Gentlemen prepare their life for their future wife.
Gentlemen desire to be strong husbands and fathers.
Gentlemen lead with love.
Gentlemen respect themselves.
Gentlemen treat women like queens.
Gentlemen are leaders.
Gentlemen are readers.
Gentlemen build their brothers.
Gentlemen strengthen their sisters.
Gentlemen express love to one another.

CHAPTER 8

Date for Data

*You can have all of the information about someone,
but only God can give you insight and revelation.*

How do you develop a relationship, in a social media age, when people would rather look at their screen than your smile? They would rather download an app, than order an appetizer with you on a date. Choose to "Netflix and chill" instead of develop ideas to network and build. Some on Instagram just want instant gratification. Others don't know how to interact face-to-face and just hide behind their Facebook page. Some people will even be more loyal to the bylaws of a phone contract, than to a marital commitment. It's enough to drive anyone crazy and give up on dating.

TRADING PLACES

Today, even the roles have been reversed. These days some women are driving to pick up a man and take him on a date, just to say they have somebody. Some have even taken a knee, to propose to their love interest. We are seeing a "new normal," where women have become the hunters and men are the prey. Some men are comfortable in a place of docility, expecting a woman to chase him.

Sis, please understand that you were not born to run and chase after a man. You were created to walk with him. Now, that doesn't mean to have the disposition of not talking to a man at all. Communicating doesn't mean you're chasing. Making conversation can elicit one's interest. If he doesn't catch the clue to pursue you, then he's not for you. Anyone that you run after, is someone who you will run away. If you're chasing them, please believe they're trying to get away. Real men don't want to be chased. They want to pursue you. Don't get in such a hurry to have somebody, that you settle for just anybody. You will never have to chase what God placed. Don't chase somebody who doesn't want to be caught. When you're chosen to receive it, you won't have to chase it. If you run after God, like you ran after that man, He will give you a man that you won't have to run after. Run after Him, not him. What is truly meant for you, won't run away from you. When you become a person of love, you will attract it. You won't have to waste time by chasing it.

What is for you, will happen for you and won't avoid you. Stop chasing and start preparing, for what you intend on attracting and receiving. You can't make anybody love you, like you, or be with you. Spare yourself the headache and heartache. Let go of what isn't meant for you, so you can receive what God has for you. Let go of what is avoiding and hurting you, even if it hurts to let go. Don't trade your self-respect for attention. Don't sacrifice your value, for someone who acts blind to you. Stay in the right place. God will give you a blessing that you won't have to chase. He chose you for the right person who will choose you. Don't lose you, by trying to choose somebody whose not for you. God will guide your purpose partner to you.

REAL EYES, REALIZE, REAL LIES

Brian Alexander the co-author of *The Chemistry Between Us: Love, Sex, and the Science of Attraction* said, "You can't determine if somebody is a potential mate by any means, other than being together and looking into their eyes." The importance of processing one's voice tone, eye contact, body language, and facial expressions are not reserved for what goes "down in the DM." It can only be ascertained through conversation. After you FaceTime, you still need some face-to-face interaction time. Not the kind that touches your body, but that which speaks to your soul, spirit, heart, and mind. In essence real eyes, realize, real truth or lies. One's real eyes are not solely what's on the outside. Real eyes have

discernment which resides on the inside. It's conveyed in

walking by faith and not by sight.

FOLLOW YOUR HEART?

People are more than what meets the eye. Pray that God

would open your spiritual eyes. When you only see with

your natural eyes, you're easy to deceive. I Samuel 16:7,

"For man looketh on the outward appearance, but the Lord

looketh on the heart." Allow God to reveal to you, who is

good for you. Don't allow your eyes, heart, and body to take

you where your mind can't keep you. People will tell you

time and time again, to follow your heart when that is not

always accurate advice.

Jeremiah 17:9 declares, "The heart is deceitful above

all things and desperately wicked: who can know it?" Don't

follow what can take you, on a detour to destruction. Never

let your eyesight cloud your insight. I'm not following my

heart, unless God speaks to my heart. Let God lead you, with every step you take and decision you make. Before you try to put a man or woman first, put God first. Keep Matthew 6:33 in view, "Seek ye first the kingdom of God and His righteousness and all these things will be added unto you."

Emotions can wreck your life and following your heart, can literally tear your life apart. Someone looking good to you is one thing, but being good for you is everything. Bro, nothing is worse than being coerced by her curves or blinded by the beauty, when on the inside she's twisted and ugly. Search for more depth, than a woman who favors Beyoncé to make your fiancé. Just because she's fine, doesn't mean she's mine. Sis, he may be handsome, but don't hang your heels on how he said "Hello." He may look like Morris Chestnut, but mentally he may be a nut. Yes, he's six feet, makes six figures, and has a six-pack. Just make sure all those sixes, don't connect you with a devil.

Don't let the fine fool you. More than what meets the

eyes attractively, you need compatibility and suitability. You've had enough physical partners. You need a purpose partner. You've had enough flesh mates. Now, you need a spirit and soulmate. Pray for discernment and direction. It will be for your protection.

INFORMATION AND REVELATION

The more you know, the better your decision making will become based upon the information you have acquired. You can have all of the information, but only God can give you revelation about a person and their situation. Everyone who is attractive to you, is not compatible with you. Is there chemistry, connectivity, and suitability? Does the person have a desire to develop and mature in God first, before trying to grow with you? Sometimes the only thing you have in common with someone is good looks. In the long run, that's not enough.

The longevity of a relationship, doesn't just revolve

around Valentine's Day or a sentimental holiday. It isn't solely immersed in grand gifts, red roses, and cards. After the roses wilt and the chocolates get stale, only real love lasts. The success of a relationship is centered around compassion, kindness, commitment, trust, and sometimes dealing with tough stuff.

A man who wants you, will do more than just text you. He will take the time to call and date you. He will do more than text "wyd" to a woman who is productive. He won't just tell you to come over or come through, but he desires to take you out and get to know you. He wants to date you, court you, and spend quality time with you. Ultimately, he will invest his time in you, if he wants to have a life with you. Don't lower your standards because you're thirsty, your biological clock is ticking, or you're entertaining thoughts of anxiety. Raise your standards because you're worthy.

DATE YOURSELF FIRST

Before you seek to find or be found by a purpose partner, make sure you take the time to date yourself first. The next person you date shouldn't be your ex and may not be the one to come next. It just might need to be yourself. If you don't know who you are, why would anyone else want to know who you are? Are you comfortable in your own company? You can really be alone and not lonely. Do you love yourself and like the skin you're in? Do you only see yourself as handsome or beautiful, when someone compliments you? Learning to love you, will protect you from those who don't value you.

Before you seek a date and desire to gain information about someone else, make sure that you first make an accurate assessment of yourself. Take the time to make an investment in yourself. Get the data on you and what God placed in you. Your goals, purpose, destiny, dreams, and vision. Go deeper beyond what people are doing socially, the hottest celebrity, and what's monetary. You can't put a price on the power of self-development via your mentality.

HIS AND HERS

Don't expect someone to do for you, what you won't do for yourself. Sis, when was the last time you bought yourself flowers and were as excited, as if someone gave them to you? Bro, when was the last time you took yourself to dinner, without a female companion? Find the value in you. Spend time getting to know you, so you don't lose yourself in someone else too.

Do you give yourself time for solitude and silence, to be introspective? Do you take the time to mute the noise around you, so you can hear God speak to you? Yes, sometimes silence can be so loud. Don't avoid it. Embrace it. Self-improvement is not only relegated to something that women should do. It's for us as men too. We must hold ourselves, to a higher level of accountability and make investments within that bring sustainability. What does it say about us as men, when women are taking courses online, if we're just sitting at home playing video games online? Too often we're playing games, while women are accomplishing goals. She can't be the only one, who is victorious and virtuous. We also have to be faithful, focused, and make progress.

QUESTIONS FOR DIRECTION

As men, we know the data on our favorite athletes and teams. We know how many touchdowns, points, assists, or rebounds a certain player or team tallied. We know how much money, we want to make and have in the bank. We know how many pushups we completed. We know how many times, we bench pressed at the gym. We know how long we ran at the track. We know the measurements of the kind of woman that appeals to our eyes. However, what are we doing to measure up to true manhood? How much time are you investing in yourself, not solely externally but internally? Are you calculating the decisions you make? Are you touching down, to tap into the real you? Not how people think of you, but the authenticity of you.

What personal points have you itemized, to address and confess? From your childhood, to your attitude, and the need for greater gratitude. Who are you assisting and who is assisting you? Are you rebounding from relationship to relationship and playing games? Will you pause, reflect, and take the time to listen to your heavenly coach? These kinds of questions, will give you and I direction. As I'm writing to you, I'm also helping me too. I don't want to be a husband who is unprepared, for my future wife who is prepared.

PICTURE PERFECT?

Our technology driven society, has us swiping and searching. Looking and liking, but not finding and loving. Comparing, competing, enhancing, and filtering but not knowing and developing who we are internally. More than what you post online for people to see, everyone is not who they "post" to be. You see the pictures of others, but what about the one of yourself? Do your strengths or struggles frame it? Look beyond the data and seek God for direction. He will give you discernment. Don't explore what you should ignore. Pray on it and recognize the signs. Too many times in relationships, we're running red lights and stopping on green ones.

Something is wrong, if we know the data on our phones, more than we know the data on ourselves. Your phone can't be the only thing, that's charged and receives power. What are you charging and changing in your life? Who and what is your power source? God's power must be the cauldron that enkindles your flame. You've downloaded apps, but what are you uploading and applying to your life? The books you read, family, friends, fitness, nutrition, mental health and wellness, should add to the holistic well-being of who you are. What good is it to know someone and they know you, but you don't know you? When you've taken the time to heal, prepare, and wait then it qualifies you to date.

You can now date with direction and purpose, by using that data to make an informed decision. In other words, seek to get information. Don't become Inspector Gadget or the FBI. Just learn to observe, communicate, and listen. Don't become so on edge or desperate, that you're seeking to get married on the first date. Before trying to jump the broom, use that same broom to sweep up the dust from your past.

CONFORMED OR TRANSFORMED?

Romans 12:2 declares, "And be not conformed to this world: but be ye transformed by the renewing of your mind." If your mind has not been renewed or transformed by God's

Word, then you will remain conformed to the world. I must allow God to lead me, so He can perfect my life daily. Indeed and in fact, none of us are perfect but all of us should be genuine.

God will never bring anyone into your life, that divides you from your destiny. They will either add to or multiply your purpose. If they are trying to divide you from your destiny, then subtract them from your life. Genesis 1:28 declares, "Be fruitful and multiply." Every person in your life should be able to do one equation and that is multiply your life. The wrong people will subtract or divide from it. The right ones will add to and multiply it.

Every man wants a woman whose presence says, "I'm not needy, I'm needed." However, a woman wants a man where she can say, "He can lead me and I don't have to lead him." Her submission to you, will be based on executing the vision God gave you. Her submission doesn't mean she's subservient. It confirms that your union complements each other, as purpose partners toward the same mission. Far too often, we only focus on what we can do for somebody or what they can do for us. The best angle of approach is what can you do with me? Can you communicate with me? Can you pray with me, grow with me, and build with me?

CONNECTED AND DISCONNECTED

The meaning of real love, seems to be lost in a "like me" generation. People will tweet and text, but won't talk. They will send you an emoji, but won't express their emotions. They will block you, quicker than they will bless you. They desire likes on Instagram, but won't express love to the common woman and man. They will post on Facebook, but won't read with their face in a book. They can share a story on Snapchat, but don't know their personal narrative. We are more connected than ever before, but arguably more disconnected than ever before.

SAME ISSUE, DIFFERENT FACE TOO

Some people are in a new relationship with the same old person. Sadly, the only thing that changed was the face. Who you're attracting has more to do with you, than it has to do with them.

You will attract the same type of person, if you're the same type of person. The quality of person that you're attracting will change, when you change. In essence, you will attract who and what you are in life. The truth is a hard pill to swallow and many will not digest it easily.

You will attract people of value, when you invest in yourself beyond what the eyes can see. Recognize your value and know your worth. Take inventory of your life and analyze it. Relationships are the glue for life. Don't get stuck with the wrong one. If you're a hater, bitter, negative, mean, and nasty person, then those are the kinds of people that you will attract.

An aphorism suggests, "We don't attract what we

want. We attract what we are." If you're attracting the same old person, it's because you're the same old person. When you're a genuine person, you attract genuine people.

Do your relationships continue to fail? Do people mistreat you, fool you, bruise you, and leave you broken? You have to get to a point where you ask yourself, "Why are all of these different people, doing the same thing to me?" Realize that it has nothing to do with them and it has everything to do with you.

TRICK OR TREAT

The way people treat you, is based on the permission that you grant them in your relationships. Yes, people may enable and mistreat you. Ultimately, it boils down to whether you deny or allow it to happen. They will never treat you right, if you keep allowing them to trick you.

Yes, everybody plays the fool, but the tragedy is remaining a fool. Don't let anybody cast you, to play the fool in your own Lifetime movie. Every lesson is a blessing, so learn from your mistakes. If you keep making the same mistake, then it's no longer a mistake but a decision.

The right choice for you, will continue to choose you. Not only with their words, but in how they treat you. When they look at you, they will see the best in you because they want the best for you. What hurt you before, doesn't compare to the best that's in store. God is getting you ready to receive, what He has ready for you. This time you're going to fall in love with someone who will catch you. They will lift you, love you, and continue to choose you. More than just anyone, real love will connect you with the right someone.

MIXED SIGNALS

I was driving the other day and noticed a car at a stop sign, with their turn signal pointed left. All of a sudden, the driver of the vehicle turned right. I laughed to myself because the driver couldn't make up their mind, thereby confusing me and others on the road.

How many times are people just like that driver? They will point you one way, but go in the opposite direction. However, it's no laughing matter when someone who you think is going to ride with you, takes another route away from you.

James 1:8 declares, "A double minded man is unstable in all his ways." Don't allow their instability, to put you in a place of insecurity. You don't need people in your life, who give you mixed signals. You need stability, not hesitation or probability. Recognize the signals and signs. Open your eyes, so you're not blind to what isn't good for you. Either they want you or they don't. Just make sure they don't stand in the way of someone who does. Either they're all in or out. Don't let somebody straddle the fence in your life.

Without question, God is connecting you with the right love that you won't have to question. Real love will give you the answers you've been looking for, in more ways than you can ask for. You don't have to look for love. It will locate you. Get ready to receive a blessing, that you won't have to question. It will be real and true. This time you won't have to ask how, what, where, and why because real love will create a way. Sis, get ready for the right man to pop the question, you're the answer and the right man's blessing!

KNOW WHAT YOU WANT

If you don't know what you want, people will decide what you get. It's worth knowing your value and it's worth knowing what you want too. A lot of people fall into one or all of three categories below. Do any of these fit you?

1. Those who don't know what they want.

2. Those who don't get what they want.

3. Those who know what they want and when they get it, they don't want it.

1. Those who don't know what they want.

One thing you have to know is what you want. Whether that's a career, relationship, or simply ordering from the menu at dinner. If you're indecisive, someone will make a decision for you. The decision will generally be what you don't want, because you haven't expressed what you do want. How do you know what you don't want, if you don't know what you do want? Are you confused yet? Well, so is the person who doesn't know what they want. Avoid the confusion by making a decision.

So you say, "Well, I just want someone to love me and treat me like a queen." Okay, so the man showed up to do both of those things, but you didn't want him. A lot of times we are indecisive because we fear rejection. We don't want to hurt others, but we don't want to be hurt either. So, be cause we have been hurt, our guard is up and now we're suspicious of everybody. As you're suspicious of others, they become suspicious of you and the cycle continues.

2. Those who don't get what they want.

You say, "Well I know what I want, but I'm not getting it."

Why? What are you doing that is preventing you from

attaining it? You will continue to get what you don't want,

if you keep focusing on what you don't want. I get it. You

don't want to be hurt or taken for granted. No one wants to

be. However, if that's all you focus on that's all you're going

to attract. What you're attracting is directly connected to

what you're focusing on. Change your focus and you will

change what you attract.

3. Those who know what they want and when they get it, they don't want it.

If you're looking for an excuse, you will find one. If you're

looking for the imperfections in others, you will find those

too. While we're looking at everyone else's imperfections,

we seemingly glance over our own and remain blind to what we do. You may say, "I want someone who is in shape, has a million dollars, a mansion, and drives a foreign car." Well, do you have any of that? What shape are you in financially, mentally, physically, and spiritually? Essentially, what are you bringing to the table, other than an appetite? If you don't know your value, what you want, or what you bring to the table then you will find yourself on someone's menu.

COURTING FOR COMMITMENT

You can't have a relationship without first building a friendship. Don't rush the process of getting to know someone. If it's logical, you're prayerful, and feelings are mutual then the prospect for dating can commence. Everyone who is dating, doesn't have intentions of marrying. This is why discernment, communication, and attaining data is key.

Courting encompasses intentionality, maturity, and

commitment for a healthy marriage. Dating helps you discern if the person is the one. Courtship provides direction to prepare for life with the one. The power of courting and committing is deciding to walk by faith, honor God, and have a relationship that is aligned His way. Courting is not solely about having a cuddle buddy, during cuffing season. If so, make sure you're boo'd up with someone who is prayed up. Dating and courting for commitment is about keeping God as the centerpiece of your relationship. It's rooted in purposeful partnership and covenant companionship with one another. The right one won't only want to date you, but they will desire to court you. They intend on marrying you.

CHAPTER 9

Issues, Issues...It's You!

*Pointing the blame will make you remain,
where you were never intended to stay.*

I f you don't have any issues, then stop reading this book. Just close it and move on with your life because of your pristine perfection. If you're still here with me, then we're in this thing together. Simply because confession is good for the soul.

I'm not perfect and neither are you, but that's not an excuse for giving up. We must strive to grow daily. The greatest growth and change, comes from recognizing our flaws and being inspired to get better each day. How can you change what you won't confront? How can you heal from it, if you won't deal with it?

BE HUMBLE

Just when you think you have it all together, life will knock you off your high horse. It will let you know that you're still human and you have plenty of room to grow. Proverbs 16:18, affirms, "Pride goeth before destruction and an haughty spirit before a fall." Indeed the climb to success is challenging, but the fall from grace can be tragic.

Reminding you to "be humble" is about more than listening to a Kendrick Lamar song. You can either be humble or be humbled. I Corinthians 10:12 affirms, "Let him who think he stands, take heed lest he fall." We must pay attention, take note, and take inventory of our lives. We must courageously face the issues that we deal with and seek to heal from them. We all have issues. Not dealing with them becomes a greater issue, which complicates our lives and those who are in it.

Your bruises and scars are battle wounds. It shows you've been in a fight, but persevered to emerge victorious.

Yes, you and I have been knocked down, but we're still here because we didn't stay down.

S.O.S.

I know you have an "S" on your chest, because you see yourself as Superman or Superwoman. Yet beyond the surface that we see with our eyes, there's an S.O.S. tattooed on our hearts. The S.O.S. of *Save Our Souls*, speaks to a quest for the remedy from the pain of the past. The past pain often blurs the vision of our future. Yes, you may have been hurt, abused, neglected, and disrespected, but you don't have to settle for less. You don't have to engage in self-destructive behaviors, that offset the destined path of purpose for your future.

Yes, we all have issues. I'm a living witness that God has the healing tissues for our hurting issues. Jeremiah 8:22, declares, "Is there no balm in Gilead? Is there no physician there? Why then is there no healing for the wound of my people?" God has the balm for our bruises and brokenness. The antiseptic of His anointing, can heal every situation and malady. His tender loving care can lift every burden, if we cast our cares on Him.

FROM A GREAT MESS TO GREATNESS

Recorded in the Synoptic Gospels of Matthew, Mark, and Luke is the story of the woman with the issue of blood. It's interesting that her affliction was public, but her name was private. Imagine going through life, being known for what happened to you and the negative experiences that you've been through.

Your mess overrides the true message of your life. Would you want to be known as the woman with the issue of abuse, neglect, or bad relationships? How about being known as the man with the issue of unemployment, addiction, or incarceration? Like me, I'm sure you would not want to be known for your issues. Your circumstances would precede the powerful person that you are from within.

A particular passage in Matthew 9:20, 21 declares, "And, behold, a woman, which was diseased with an issue of blood twelve years, came behind Him (Jesus), and touched the hem of His garment. For she said within herself, If I may but touch His garment, I shall be whole."

The woman had an issue of blood for twelve years. We may not have the same particular issue that she had, but many times we carry our burdens and issues for years. Oftentimes we go through life broken, hurt, angry, depressed, confused, and lacking love within ourselves. Imagine being in this woman's shoes. Under the Mosaic law, she was deemed to be unclean. She was not allowed to come in contact with anyone or they would be classified as unclean too. Still, she pressed her way through the crowd to Jesus. Despite what you're going through or what you've been through, keep pressing your way to Jesus. Don't let people block you or stop you, from getting close to Him.

YOU HAVE THE RIGHT TOUCH

She didn't touch Jesus, but she touched something that was touching Him. She touched the hem of His garment. There was enough power to transition her from sickness to healing. She had enough faith to push through her pain, to experience the power of deliverance. It doesn't matter how long you've been carrying around your particular issue(s). If you take it to God, He will empower you to handle it and find healing.

There are countless accounts of healing in the Bible. It's interesting some men were healed, as Jesus would restore their sight/vision. Every man must have a vision for his life, because it impacts one's relationships and the decisions they make. If you have sight but no vision, then you're still blind.

I CAN SEE CLEARLY NOW

Brother, if we walk through life being blinded by our issues, we will never be the conduits of power in our communities. A man with vision is gifted by God to produce, protect, and provide for the people in his life. Take off the blinders and remove the mask, so you can walk boldly into your future with vision.

You may be asking, "How can I deal with my issues of abandonment, abuse, neglect, unsuccessful relationships, depression, disappointment, the secret pains, and hurts?" Nobody seems to hear my silent screams. Well, the Bible is full of individuals with issues who found remedies:

THE WOMAN AT THE WELL

John chapter 4 highlights the woman at the well, who had five husbands. Also, the man she was living with was not her husband. Jesus did not approach her to spit game, but He came to restore and give her living water. She was drawing from a physical well, but He wanted her spiritual well to never run dry again.

MIGHTY GOOD MAN

The woman left her water pot, went into the city and said, "Come, see a man, who told me all things I ever did: is not this the Christ?" The Hip-Hop group, Salt-N-Pepa would say, "What a man, what a man, what a mighty good man."

Sis, a man is mighty good when he can speak life, into your life and his actions align with his words. Don't make the mistake of only evaluating him, by how much money is in his pocket. Seek to draw from the wealth and value, in his mind and heart.

Don't get caught up in what car he drives. Find out what path he's driving to. Don't let him drive you into a life of hell, drama, and abuse. Yes, I know he can pay for you, but will he pray with and for you? Discover his ambitions, what motivates him, and his vision. Focus more on becoming the right woman for the right man, instead of settling for a man right now.

My brother, make sure that you look beyond her voluptuous body. Find out if her lifestyle, aligns with your core values. You must allow God to give you vision, to see beyond what you see. You need more than a flesh mate or a soulmate. You need a spirit mate. What your spirit needs, is greater than what your flesh desires. The right one will awaken the vision, dream, and spirit in you. Not just temporarily but permanently.

THE CRIPPLED WOMAN

In Luke chapter 13, the woman in the story could not straighten her body, look upward, or forward. The shape of her body was bent toward the ground for 18 years. Imagine having to walk bent over for 18 years, much less 18 minutes.

I've had back pain on a number of occasions and if your body is bent over, then you know it feels horrendous. Thankfully, my chiropractor gave me relief. However, it's another thing to deal with that kind of pain for 18 years.

As it was, she could only see the dirt at her feet. She could only look downward and see the bad side of things. She couldn't look up and see the possibilities before her. She could not see the smiles on people's faces. She could not see the sky. She could only see the dirt. So often, we look at the dirt of our circumstances and decisions, but God will change your view and bring restoration to you.

Sometimes life brings you so low, that all you trust is the dust. The cards of life can deal you a bad hand, to where you become pessimistic instead of optimistic. Despite what you have experienced, shake it off. Just because it's been that way, doesn't mean it will stay that way. You can change your circumstance, by thinking positive in a negative situation.

HEAVY HEART, HEAVY ISSUES

Can you imagine this woman's condition? She couldn't look up, due to being bent over. Sometimes our issues weigh us down, to where even our physical body is impacted. How we feel on the inside, will impact our body and expression on the outside.

Whatever is going on in our mind will manifest throughout our body. You can only smile through pain for so long, before you break down. They say, "Fake it until you make it." However, you won't truly make it, if you have to continually fake it. Rather, "Faith it until you make it." Believe and walk by faith. Fear paralyzes you, but faith mobilizes you. When you become real with your issues, you will seek relief. Sometimes it takes being sick and tired of being sick and tired, to find healing.

When Jesus saw her condition, He told her that she was free. She was free from the infirmity that twisted her body. Even as you're reading, the Lord is freeing and healing you from every situation that you're going through. Jesus declared, "Woman, thou art loosed from thine infirmity." Jesus laid His hands on her. Immediately, she straightened her body and was made whole.

HANDS OF HEALING

Sis, a Godly and respectful man, won't use his hands to hurt or harm you. He will stretch his hands to heal and help you. The woman with the issue of infirmity, received her healing. She could look upward and forward. It was not just her body that was healed, but her heart. She praised God because of it. Her brokenness became her breakthrough. God can heal you and change your outlook on life. When He frees you, nothing can keep you bound!

For 18 years, the woman could only look downward. Since she was healed, her eyes could look upward. She could not only see the sun, but she could see the Son. Wherever you're looking, is an indication of where you're going. Are you looking back at your past or focused on your future? Look ahead and allow God to strengthen you. Let your eyes and mind be the engine that propels you, on the path toward your purpose. Keep your eyes to the skies. The sky is not the limit for you, it's just a view. Psalm 121:1

declares, "I will lift up my eyes unto the hills, from which comes my help. My help comes from the Lord, who made heaven and earth."

THE CANAANITE WOMAN

Recorded in Matthew 15:21-28, is the story of a Canaanite woman, who had a daughter that was demonically possessed. She came and fell down at Jesus' feet. According to customs, they were not supposed to communicate. Simply because Jesus was a Jew and Biblical scholars suggest, the woman from Canaan was black.

AIN'T TOO PROUD TO BEG

The woman begged Jesus to cast the demon out of her daughter. He replied to her, "Let the children first be filled: for it is not meet for me to take the children's bread, and to cast it unto the dogs." Maybe you missed it but Jesus referred to the woman as a dog. Many would regard that connotation as offensive. I know a few people, who would've given Jesus a piece of their mind. They would say, "Hold up, I'm from the east side. Jesus you called me a what?"

However, as bold as Jesus' statement was, the woman's reply was even bolder. She said, "Yes, Lord: yet the dogs under the table eat of the children's crumbs." The woman could have expressed that she was offended. Rather she looked past the offense and received her breakthrough. So much so, that even her statement made the Lord holler. Jesus said, "O woman, great is your faith. Be it unto you as thou wilt" and her daughter was immediately healed.

I'M THROUGH WITH ISSUES

It's quite interesting, none of these individuals with issues and sisters with struggles had their names mentioned. Their issues outwardly seemed to outweigh who they were inwardly. I can hear people now, "Look, that's the woman who got a divorce. This is the woman who lost her house or whose child is on drugs. There she is, there she goes, that's her right there." Sometimes we're known more by our issues, than by the value that's infused in our spirit. Don't fret and focus on the issue. Focus on placing your issues in God's hand. The Master has a master plan.

The issues of dating, relationships, marriage, love, wholeness, and overcoming your past are small in God's hands. Maybe you're saying to yourself, "How long will I be single and when will I get married? Time is ticking and I want companionship." In your time of being alone, God seeks to make you one with Him. The issue will always look big in your hands. Place it in God's hands and He will sustain you, while He prepares what's intended for you.

In a place of singleness and solitude, is an opportunity to continue to grow and work on yourself. Many times we see it as delay or denial, when in fact it's neither. God is orchestrating the right person and opportunity, to collide with your destiny at the right timing.

HIS BEST FOR THE BEST

How can God send you the right one, if you're still connected to the wrong one? He will not release His best, if you're entangled in drama and mess. Don't settle for a momentary substitute, when God has the right attribute to fit you for a lifetime.

Do you have the discipline, to wait and go through the season(s) where God is The Potter, you are the clay, and He molds you each day? When you're the clay, you feel The Potter working on the intricate places of your life. No, it's not comfortable, but it's necessary. It doesn't feel good now, but it's going to work out for your good in the end. Trust Him through the process. Stop looking for somebody to complete you. Only God does that. He's not giving a half person, to a whole person. He wants you to be healed. God wants you to walk in wholeness, but you have to place the brokenness and shattered pieces of your life in His hands.

So often we fail to see our own brokenness, because we're pointing the finger and looking for flaws in everyone else. Before analyzing and criticizing someone else's issues, look at your own first. Sometimes we're carrying around more baggage, than the cargo on an airplane. When you go through life broken and weighed down, your dreams can't take flight. Cast your cares on God because He cares for you. Throw all of your issues at Him and He will empower you to overcome them. Where you're going to, is greater than what you're going through. The bigger the battle, the greater the blessing.

TOO LOOSED, TO BE BOUND

Jesus told the crippled woman in the book of Luke, "Woman thou art loosed." Confess over your life that you're loosed from abuse. You're loosed from your past. You're loosed from brokenness, low self-esteem, depression, bitterness, and anger. You are loosed to walk in liberty and love.

As you're reading this chapter, maybe you're saying, "Why the ladies and the accounts of women being healed?" I'm so glad that you asked. I believe there is something intrinsically special about how a woman is designed.

WAITING TO EXHALE

When God created Eve, she was never taken from the head of Adam to be superior to him. Eve was not taken from Adam's foot, to be beneath him. She wasn't even taken from his spine, to be behind him. Eve was taken from the rib of Adam's side, to surround and stand beside him.

If you study the anatomical structure of the human body, you will discover that your ribs protect your lungs which assist in breathing. Brother, when you find your rib, you will be able to breathe much easier. However, if it's the wrong one, she will give you asthma and emphysema.

Sometimes what is best for us, is right in front of our face. Yet because they don't fit our fantasy or preference, we ignore them. He may not be a millionaire, but he has the mindset of a millionaire. So, it's worth the investment. She may not look like a supermodel, but she is a role model who makes a difference.

Relationships will never flourish, if you allow your issues to consume you selfishly. Growth occurs when it's rooted in reciprocity. If you connect via vision as two become one, then you can multiply your resources by investing in one another. I'm not saying lower your standards or ideals for a relationship and marriage. Just explore them a little further. Delve a little deeper. When you understand the laws of relationships, you will realize the principles of investing in someone's value that reaps sustainable benefits.

FAITHFULLY FLAWED

Oftentimes, we have to weigh vanity versus value and substance in juxtaposition with style. Think about your flaws, in dichotomy with the flaws of others. Don't put the blame on everyone else, to where you fail to remedy your issues and grow in the process. There are no perfect people. We are imperfect people, striving for perfection. Despite your flaws you're still worth it. Remain faithful, focused, and committed to becoming a better you. As a result, you will attract the right person who is a blessing to you. Take the time to think and work through every issue. God will flip the script and use the issues that bruised you, as a catalyst for greater love and breakthroughs.

CHAPTER 10

Marriage Is a Marathon

The goal is not to just get married. It's to stay married.

The objective of holy matrimony is not simply the ceremony, it's marital unity. Yes, it's about more than a ring, proposal, engagement, and wedding. God is preparing you for a marriage. All of the above is a sprint, but two individuals becoming one is a marathon. Securing a ring, gown, and having a wedding doesn't mean it's over. This is when the real work begins. The goal should not be, to just get married. It should be to stay married. However, the caveat is that being married won't heal you and being single won't kill you. When it's in God's timing, waiting doesn't mean you're wasting your time.

MR. RIGHT OR MR. RIGHT NOW?

I was talking to a friend of mine who is in her 30s. She's never been married and has no children. As her birthday approached she said to me, "Eddie I'm trying to be ready for my Mr. Right in every category. Now, if only God will show me where he is, I'll be good to go." I listened, thought about it and replied, "Stop waiting on God to show you where he is, when God wants to show him where you are." In other words, get in position so he can find you. Not the other way around. Just because you're in your thirties, doesn't mean you have to be thirsty. Mr. Right Now won't find you, in the place where Mr. Right is praying and preparing to locate you. Do you have enough patience, to be single and selective? Will you rush and settle for what's wrong, because you think God is taking too long?

Realize as a woman, God didn't even put you on this planet until everything was in place. You are the crescendo of creation and the zenith of God's zeal. Understand that's how special you are. God brought you into order not chaos. If a man doesn't have his life in order and in place, much less his own place, then don't give him a place in your heart.

God didn't bring you into the earth realm, until everything was established. The trees, the seas, the land, the lakes, the rivers, fish, foul of the air, the animals, and ultimately a man. After everything was in place, then it was time for a woman to come to fruition. You're that special, because you are the centerpiece of creation. You're not just the decorative bow on an expensive gift. You are a gift!

Once everything was in place, then God pulled you out of the man. God is not going to give you to any random male. He wants to position you with the right man. God is connecting you with a gentleman, who will man up and lift you up.

SEND ME YOUR LOCATION

In Proverbs 18:22 "He that findeth" means one who meets, encounters, discovers, and locates. Sis, it's not your job to do the finding. You should be praying and discerning, to see the right one God is sending.

The singer Khalid said, "Send me your location, let's focus on communicating because I don't need nothing else but you." The question is what signals are you sending, for the right man to locate you? The signals encompass your character, communication, personality, work ethic, and even who you surround yourself with daily. Your purpose partner doesn't want to be with anyone else but you, because they only have eyes for you.

Men are more observant than you think they are. Yes, your voluptuous body caught our eyes. However, your inner beauty will cause us to invest our time. It provides a compass, to be in search of you and communicate with you.

A man will respect you, when you keep your standards higher than your heels. When a man finds a woman like you who is rare, nothing else can compare.

HURRY UP AND WAIT

God refuses to be rushed, despite our pouting and poor decision making. In a fast-paced, microwave, instantaneous, hot and ready society, we want things expediently. It's like the person who prayed for patience. Their prayer was "Lord give me patience now. Give it to me right now." Yes, weeping may endure for a night, but we want the joy that same night. We don't want to wait until the morning. We like destinations not journeys, highways not pathways. We want everything done in a hurry, instant gratification, and answers immediately. We don't like slow, steady, and long-suffering. We want suddenly and right now blessings. God can do that but He is also calculated.

Maybe you see everyone else getting married and ask

yourself, "When will it be my time?" You have been a groomsman and bridesmaid long enough. You have been to more weddings, than you can count. All of your girls are getting married. Your homeboys are proposing left and right. People begin to inquire and wonder, how long will you wait? Will you ever get married? As a result, you now begin to compare, question yourself, or even entertain the idea of settling. Don't sprint to get into, what is intended to be a marathon for two.

Stop focusing on what everyone is pressuring you to do. Take your ears and eyes off them. Place them on Him. Remember God's ways are not your ways and His thoughts are not your thoughts. His purposeful pace is worth your patience. What you want to last, doesn't always happen fast. God is preparing you through quiet faith, not quick fixes.

Your patience is preparing you for your promise. All of the moments of hurt, trials, isolation, rejection, and pain won't compare to your moment of joy. Everything you've hoped for, is worth you waiting for. Expect to receive more. Don't rush it. Be patient as you expect it. God will do it. The financial breakthrough, business, promotion, marriage, and blessings are still coming. Keep working the vision within you. More than just anything or something, expect God to give you everything!

RIGHT ONE, RIGHT TIME

Essentially it's better to wait long, than to marry wrong. Don't rush to get in, what you should have never been in. Don't make permanent decisions, based on temporary feelings and circumstances. You have nothing to prove to anybody. Don't just settle for anyone, so you can say you have someone. Making sure your life is in the right stage, is more important than being married by a certain age.

What's more important, being married by 30+ or staying married for 30+ years? What good is it to prepare for a wedding, but be unprepared for marriage? Waiting on God, doesn't mean you're wasting your time. When it's in His will, it will happen with the right one at the right time. Take note and be sure you're marrying the right one, so you don't have to endure the pain of divorcing the wrong one.

COLLABORATION OR COMPETITION?

You need a teammate not an opponent. The right one won't compete against you. They will collaborate with you. They realize your success is theirs too. If they see the best in you, they will want the best for you. The right one will encourage you, coach you, pray with and for you. Whoever is intimidated, will soon be eliminated. Time and time again, you've faced enough opposition. The right teammate and purpose partner, will position you to walk in victory. The one who wants the best for you will work, pray, and grow with you. Stop falling for people, who aren't capable of catching you. Make sure they have the right hands to support, love, and strengthen you. Real love will protect you, not neglect you. The right person won't hold you back. They will have your back.

MARRIAGE IS A MINISTRY

I asked a couple, who has been married for 40 years, to share some marital insight with me. They explained that the secret to staying married, is learning the art of forgiveness. They informed me that without forgiveness, a relationship will never progress. Marriage is about more than creating memories. It's a ministry. You can't come in looking to be served, like a customer. You have to serve like a waitress or waiter. The marriage won't last by being selfish. You have to be selfless.

I find it interesting that you take a test to get a driver's license, but there's no test to get a marriage license. So, essentially people learn how to drive safely, but can crash a marriage abruptly. This is why pre-marital counseling is key, if you have a vision to start the marriage ignition.

MAKE ROOM TO BLOOM

Being in a relationship or marriage won't make you happy, if you're single and miserable. Marriage is a marathon and a merger. Move from brokenness to wholeness, so God can merge you with who He has for you. Despite a broken marriage, relationship, or heart God will give you a brand new start. While you're waiting, focus on your purpose as you're preparing. You're too special to settle for just anyone. God will bless you with the right one.

Make room for something new to bloom. Clear the clutter and sweep all of the negative things out of your life. As the season of your life is changing, it's time to begin rearranging and transforming your life. Eliminate toxic relationships and stinking thinking. Remove what isn't good for you, so the right things can be added to you. It's time to bloom where you're planted!

ANSWERED PRAYER

Sis, when you place your heart in God's hands, the right man will seek God for your hand. A woman like you is rare and the answer to the right man's prayer. He knows you are worth the wait. You're the kind of wife, that will add value to his life. The right man is praying for a woman like you. He is working on himself, to be a good husband to you. Don't rush it. Rest knowing it. A precious jewel like you, will be loved by the man that God has for you. Stay ready, it's coming and it's closer than you're thinking. It will happen and be more than you can imagine. Beyond just a wedding, your marriage will be a blessing. God is connecting you two. Get ready to say "I do" to the right man, who prayed to marry you!

It's worth it, to know you're worth it. Don't let anyone diminish your value, when you know what you bring to the table. Too often we lower our expectations because of our experiences. Learn to love you, before you expect someone else to. Heal within and begin again, by recognizing your worth and value. To attract what's on a greater level, you too have to be on another level. You don't attract what you want. You attract who and what you are. Your future is waiting for you, to rise above your past.

WEAR YOUR CROWN

You're too special to settle for just anything, when you've been through everything. Look at how God has blessed you. I salute and celebrate you. What you've endured doesn't define you, it refines you. It's not what's on the outside. It's your strength on the inside that sustains you. Through the tears, you still smile. Through hurt, love flows from your heart. You're the kind of woman, who is an extraordinary queen of quality. You're the type of man who possesses kingly qualities, royally, and uniquely. Disappointment, depression, drama, and divorce could not destroy you. It unveiled the strength that God placed inside of you. He is lifting you, above what you've been through. Isaiah 62:3 reminds you, "Thou shalt also be a crown of glory, in the hand of the Lord and a royal diadem in the hand of thy God."

Yes, you've been strong for so long, but God is sending the right shoulder for you to lean on. The right man will pray with you, provide, and protect you. The right woman will crown you with love, wisdom, and honor as a gift to you. Be encouraged and don't let anything bring you down. Lift your head and wear your crown.

LET IT GO

Is loving them hurting you? Ask yourself. Just because you forgave them, doesn't mean you still have to be with them or associate with them. Stop hurting yourself, trying to fix somebody who hurt you. Love yourself enough to let it go. Stop taking people back, who keep pulling you back. It's okay to keep your distance. Forgive and love them from a distance.

Why rekindle a flame that should be extinguished? Don't go back and get the person that God delivered you from. God brought you out of it. Forgive, move forward, and don't look back at it. A toxic relationship is a biohazard to your blessings. God won't bless mess. You can't move forward, going backward. In order to grow, you must love yourself enough to let go.

God won't send you the right one, until you let go of the wrong one. You can't move forward with people, who only want to go in circles. Marriage is a merger and a marathon, to progress not regress. Make sure you make the right investment, with the one that God has for you or they will bankrupt you. Not just financially but emotionally, mentally, and spiritually. The wrong love, isn't love at all. Love yourself enough to walk away, so God can make a way.

ONE WITH THE RIGHT ONE

Start preparing for what God has prepared. He is going to make you one with the right one. As you become one with God, you will become one with who He has for you. Don't give up on love. Remain confident that your prayers will be answered and your desires will be granted. More than a wedding, expect a marriage that is built on a firm foundation of faith, love, honesty, and integrity.

Your knight in shining armor, will honor the queen in you. God is directing the steps you are taking. The right one is coming to change your last name and address, with a ring and a vision to be your lifetime blessing. The two of you will become one. Your purpose partner will count the ways of how your love makes them amazed. Just like a Brian McKnight song, "One, you're like a dream come true. Two, just want to be with you. Three, girl it's plain to see that you're the only one for me." Realize that you're made for what you've prayed for, which is the best and that much more!

QUALITY OVER QUANTITY

A woman who possesses the qualities of a wife, is a purpose partner for life. She serves God and her community. She brings peace not pressure. She is the kind of spouse, who has order in her house. She speaks words of life. She lives virtuously with purity. She is confident and clothed in strength. She is not a liability but an asset. Her beauty inside, far exceeds what's on the outside. She is purpose driven, in preparation for her spouse.

A man who has the qualities of a husband, is a covenant companion. He listens as God leads him. He has a vision and takes action. He is disciplined in mind, body, and spirit. He prays, protects, and works to provide. He possesses strength to love. He elevates his woman. He speaks to the queen in her. He is a gentleman, who leads with integrity and walks in purity. He does not avoid self-development. He works daily to make improvements.

His life reflects one of respectability and responsibility. He

is active in his community. He uplifts the people in his life.

He surrounds himself with wise counsel. He is preparing his

life, for his wife.

CONFIDENT CONNECTION

Be confident in knowing, that God is connecting you with

who He has for you. While you're waiting, God is working.

Remain focused and keep working. Don't rush and make the

wrong choice, by leaning to your own understanding. Let

God take care of it, so you don't have to recover from it.

More than a wedding, God is preparing you for the right

marriage. The right one will be your peace, not your

pressure. They will be your blessing, not your stressing.

They will embrace you, because they will never be able to

replace you. Get ready! You have the victory. What you've

prayed for is coming. Stay ready and remain under God's

covering. You will be covered with healing, encouragement, respect, affection, protection, prayer, and tender loving care.

LIVING MY BLESSED LIFE

Don't let the pain from an ex, prevent you from receiving the love from the right one next. Your future of favor, is greater than your past pain. Refuse to be bitter. Know that better is coming. Bless and release them. When you're healed, you won't wish hell upon them. You will wish well for them. When you find the good in goodbye, you can look back and laugh at the past. In you they lost the best, but it was a setup to receive the blessed.

Just because you're grown, doesn't mean you stop growing. Keep blooming into the woman that you're becoming. Continue to position yourself, as a man on a mission. What you're about to gain, is greater than what you gave up, to get where you're going. The disappointment, isolation, and rejection prepared you for a greater purpose.

You've perfumed your pain and masked it with makeup. You've smiled through the tears, but God will restore your years. What it cost you, doesn't compare to your priceless value. Queen, keep wearing your crown and blooming where you're planted. King, recognize the greatness in yourself and don't settle for less. You're strong enough, to survive tough times to become the man, woman, son, daughter, father, mother, husband, and wife to live your blessed life!

SEE IT, SEIZE IT

If they see you as a husband or wife, they won't play with your heart, but will make you a part of their life. Sometimes life has dealt you a bad hand, where you only choose from deficits rather than assets. Let God remove what isn't good for you, so He can match you with what's best for you. The next person you select, won't be out of need. It will be where God leads. Where God guides, He always provides. Let God do the shuffling, subtracting, and adding. You will receive your lifelong blessing.

You've had enough tears. Get ready to laugh again. You've had enough pain. Get ready for a power encounter. You've had enough people, withdraw from you and leave you bankrupt. Get ready to make an investment that lasts forever. Prepare and position yourself in the right place. For every joker, you're going to have the last laugh. Your king and queen connection, will be blessed and built to last.

For all of the times you've been praying, hoping, and expecting, just know that your blessing is coming. God will do, what He said He will do. Eyes haven't seen and ears haven't heard, what God is getting ready to do for you. The blessing will transform your home, relationships, finances, marriage, business, and ministry. Get ready to glow up! God is about to blow your mind and show up. Open your eyes of faith. See it before you see it, so you can seize it!

ROYALTY DEMANDS LOYALTY

Beyond what is on you, the right man will see the value in you. More than your assets, He recognizes that you are an asset to his life. Your union will encompass love, faith, provision, protection, and strong communication. Your king will look past your past, because He wants to build a future with you. You're the type of woman, who a man will thank God for your existence. I'm talking about marrying, changing your last name, address, and finishing each other's sentence. You have "wife" written all over you, but some men can't read. Sis, if he's blind to your value, then he's not for you.

A man doesn't need a wife, until he has order in his life. He should not come for you, until he does what he's supposed to do. He doesn't want to solely chase you. He wants to be chaste with you. As he pursues you, it's in purity that's purpose driven, according to God's plan for you. The right man will pursue you, like he's still trying to get you, when he already has you. Even after he marries you, he still wants to date you. He knows you're the kind of queen and wife, who complements his life. He only has eyes for you, to honor you royally with his loyalty!

ARE YOU DISMISSIVE OR SUBMISSIVE?

Like a rib protects the heart, a wife protects her husband. A husband also protects his wife, in the same manner. They submit to one another as unto God. Are you dismissive or submissive though? The prefix "sub" means under. How can you expect someone to submit to you if you're negative, nasty, or a nag? Do you have an understanding of one another, to submit to one another? Essentially, are you a headache or a helpmate?

Ephesians 5:21 declares, "Submitting yourselves one to another in the fear of God." The suffix of "ing" means to submit continually, by doing it over and over again. Ephesians 5:22, 23, and 25 affirms, "Wives, submit yourselves unto your own husbands, as unto the Lord. For the husband is the head of the wife, even as Christ is the head of the church: and He is the savior of the body. Husbands, love your wives, even as Christ also loved the church and gave Himself for it."

A husband who is the head of his household, will love his wife as Christ loved the church. As the head, he is the covering. He stands in front of the storm, so you don't feel the ramifications of it. He will pray for you, provide, protect, and love you. Submission in marriage honors God.

There are couples who have been married for years, but are still not husband and wife. They are more like roommates. Legally they have the title. Lovingly they don't function in the position, due to a lack of submission.

As a wife, submission honors and affirms your husband's leadership. Just as he affirms the gifts that you bring as a helpmate. Understand, if serving and submitting is below you, then marriage is beyond you. One person is not inferior to the other. However, submission is two-fold, as each one submits to the other. Submission does not mean control. Submission doesn't mean, put a tether on somebody. Submission isn't manipulative or controlling. It doesn't make you a private investigator, to keep someone under surveillance. It doesn't even MapQuest their every move. Real love and submission doesn't restrain you from doing wrong. It constrains you to do right. You can't submit to any person, unless you first submit to God.

MARRIAGE OR MIRAGE?

Poet and playwright Robert Browning declared, "Success in marriage is more than finding the right person. It is being the right person." Marriage will always be a mirage, if you compare your spouse or what you think someone has in contrast to your house. Marriage is not momentary, but designed for longevity. One must take serious precaution and preparation. Don't leap so quickly, that you end up limping drastically. God must lead you via prayer, patience, and preparedness.

IT TAKES THREE

As a couple, the man makes up one side and the woman makes up the other side of a marriage. In unity, their bond creates a circle. The only way to fill that circle is with Christ. In this case, three is not company. It is complete and divine unity, symbolic of the trinity. A complete relationship includes three: God, you, and your spouse. Don't allow opinions, distractions, or naysayers to infiltrate your covenant circle. Marriage is a joint effort that will only work, if you both work together with God. It truly takes three to bring marital and spiritual unity.

IF YOU DON'T MIND

Don't trip and lose your mind over what you've lost. You're going to need your mind for what's to come. Don't lose your mind over a bad relationship. You're going to need your mind to sustain a good marriage. Don't lose your mind, over the one who didn't see your value. You're going to need your mind, for the one who will celebrate you.

Don't lose your mind, over the people who treated you negatively. You're going to need your mind to think positively. Don't lose your mind over the past. You're going to need your mind, to step into your future. Don't lose your mind over the wrong one. You're going to need your mind, to walk in wholeness with the right one.

Don't lose your mind, over the person who left your house. You're going to need your mind, for the spouse who will create a home with you. Don't lose your mind, over the one who wants to play. You're going to need your mind, for the one who respects you and desires to stay.

Tell the wrong one never mind. You've changed your mind. Don't pay your past any mind. Just make up your mind to walk in your destiny. Prepare for your spouse that God has prepared and designed with you in mind.

HANDS OF YOUR HUSBAND

Your heart won't be in the hands of any man, only your husband. Everything you've been through was preparing you, for this year that God has for you. All along God was preparing the man he has for you, to be a good husband to you. Keep your heart in God's hands. The right man will seek God's heart to have your hand. He will love you, pray with you, and protect your heart in his hands. More than a wedding, God is aligning you at the right timing for the right marriage.

Presently prepare for your spouse and the future you both will share. Don't fight it or doubt it. This will be the year that God does it! See it before you see it, so you can receive it. Get ready for your wedding ring, which will be all in God's timing. A good woman like you, is deserving of a good man who will love, respect, and protect your heart in his hands. Trust God's process. He will give you His best.

Start practicing and preparing to say, "I do" to the one who is sent by God to love you!

WIFE YOU, RENAME YOU

Marriage is more than a contract, it's a covenant. Your future husband wants to change two things about you: your last name and your address. Just like the singer Tank, you can take that to the bank. The right man will "wife you and rename you." Get ready to be addressed, as "Mrs." because you're deserving of the best.

Your husband will be impressed by your heart, not just your hips. The most important curve is the smile on your lips. He will love you and bring out the best in you. For all of the stress you went through, God is sending the right person that will bless and build with you. Start preparing for what God is preparing for you. The tears of joy on your face, will replace the hurt in your heart and pain of your past. Expect a real love that lasts. Queen, place your heart in

God's hand and He will put it in a king's hand who will love, provide, protect, and respect you. Know that you are the answer, to the right man's prayer. He won't prey on you. He will pray with and for you.

Yes, your curves will attract him, but only character will keep him. On the outside is what will attract a man to you. However, who you are on the inside will keep him with you. A man who is faithful to God, will be faithful to you. He's working and praying, to be a good husband to a good woman like you. For all of your pain through the years, get ready to experience joyful tears.

MARRYING HAS A TIMING

What is a ring, if it's not the right person and the wrong timing? Understand that timing is everything. The love you've been expecting is coming. Prepare and stay ready. God will position you, for the right one that He has for you. The mistakes you've made and the lessons learned, have prepared you. Expect the best and a blessing that's priceless. Remember what's for you is for you. There is no need to compete for love or devalue yourself to receive it. The right man is looking for a wife, who adds value to his life. He will also add value to hers in return. He sees in you, what others were blind to. Let Him find you, working the vision that God gave you. As you're believing and preparing, know that your king is coming. He will marry you at the right time and love you for a lifetime.

YOUR NEXT IS NOW

God is flipping the script and turning the line around. Your next is about to happen now. It seems like you were last, but you're about to be first. The blessing that's meant for you, didn't pass you. It's being prepared with tender loving care for you. So many times you've asked, "When will it be my turn and my time?" You've created a vision board to envision your purpose partner. You think of a future with them often. You've prayed and cried over it. You've even thought that you missed your time. Know that God has aligned it. You're right on time for His assignment. Start rejoicing because of it. Don't compare, compete, or complain. Your next chapter, will be greater than your last one. Your next relationship and marriage, will be better than your last one. More than finding the right one, it's time to become the right one. The next idea, project, woman, or man will be led by God's plan. Your next is now. What you've prayed, cried, and believed for is about to happen suddenly. God is turning the line around. You thought you were last, but God will make you first. Get ready to receive what He has for you now, because you're next!

CHAPTER 11

Husband with a Vision

Expect provision as a covenant companion,
to lead and love your wife as a husband.

I asked a question earlier in the book, "Who is teaching our boys and men to be husbands?" We do a good job of preparing women to be virtuous wives. However, who is teaching us to be faithful husbands? Are we preparing women to marry men, who aren't prepared for marriage? It's something to give thought and consideration to. Much of the relationship rules for dating and marriage are directed to women. Admittedly, I too have been an ambassador of that rhetoric. Not from the standpoint of sharing in error, but I recognize the need for balance. As men, we can't hold women to a standard that we are not capable of attaining ourselves. In many cases, the standard should be higher for us, than what we perpetuate upon women.

Ironically this is Chapter 11. Oftentimes, as men we have filed for chapter 11 bankruptcy emotionally, financially, psychologically, and spiritually. All due to the delinquency, of our respectability and responsibility. Through it all, I still believe that God is calling single men, fathers, and husbands to a greater standard of accountability and authenticity. Then and only then, can we gain respectability and harness our leadership ability. We can't be savages, by running through the streets and expect women to just be bookworms at home. The same onus that we place on her, should also be placed on ourselves.

PAPA WAS A ROLLING STONE

It's easy to be counterproductive and play the blame game. Especially, if there was no father in your life or you didn't have a great example of one. Just because Papa was a rolling stone, doesn't mean you have to be. The generational curse of alcoholism, poverty, incarceration, promiscuity, and irresponsibility may run in your family. However, it should run out with you. Yes, we are born looking like our parents, but we live and die looking like our decisions.

PRESENTLY ABSENT

The issue of responsibility, still hits home to me and is personalized. If you were like me, you grew up in a single parent home. My mother did her very best, in trying to navigate the role of mother and "father." When in actuality, no parent can ever play both roles. I do have to give mom her props though. She taught me a multiplicity of life lessons to love God, respect myself, and help others. She even taught me how to dribble a basketball, kick a football, and would even stand in front of the door until I opened it for her. Mom taught me how to be a gentleman. She affirmed that my treatment of her, is a blueprint for how I will treat a woman and future wife. If a man won't love, honor, and respect his own mother. He won't love, honor, and respect his woman or wife either.

Prior to my parents' divorce, my father was in the house for a period of time. However, when he was there, he wasn't there. Have I lost you? When he was present physically he was absent mentally, emotionally, relationally, and spiritually.

As a young boy, I witnessed and endured the absence of my father from our household. I was perplexed, being faced with abandonment and rejection. Imagine the scars left on a child's life, who is searching for identity in society without proper rearing. You can't help but to ask, "What did I do wrong, for you to leave? Am I not the son you wanted? Am I not worthy of love?"

So, like many fatherless young men today, I looked for a father figure on TV or in the streets. However, athletes, actors, and celebrities couldn't fill the void. I tried to cover the hurt, through my friends and use sports as a bandaid for the hemorrhaging pain. I looked to Michael Jordan, as a "father figure" on television. I admired his perseverance, tenacity, and competitive drive. Not even Jordan's aerial artistry could soothe my apathy, calm my fears, or wipe away the tears.

Maybe you have asked, "How can I be responsible, if I never saw it exemplified in a man?" Now, as the father removes himself from the mother and child's life, it leaves a feeling of being rejected in their lives. As a result, children begin to appropriate rejection in many forms, whether psychologically, emotionally, or spiritually. Many begin to act out or rebel, because all they know is hurt. So, it begins to replicate in our relationships. The hurt manifests through physical or verbal abuse, inadequacy, and a lack of responsibility.

As men we love to plant the seed, but tending the soil is where we have our hang ups. Some of the abuse at the hands of others, is replicated into promiscuity and enraptured in a psychological conundrum. The one who should be there to protect, must not neglect. They should help to heal, not cause one's hurt. Seemingly, the sins of the father have revisited their sons.

WHAT'S UP MAN?

Much like Psalm 27:10, I can truly say, "When my father left me, then the Lord took me up." God is lifting you above your circumstances and previous experiences. Without a doubt, being a man in today's world, presents its fair share of challenges. We are often hit hard with hurdles.

From the onset of conception, we internalize traits by which we were taught to parade our masculinity. We echo in our deep vibrato, "Yeah, I'm a man." We act as if we came into this world as men of steel. We behave as if we're so tough, that when we were born, we didn't even cry. We often think that our power, is portrayed in our physical array and display of strength. A false sense of masculinity is minimized, by what's on the outside. True power is maximized, by what you possess on the inside. For "Greater is He that is in you, than he that is in the world" (I John 4:4).

As men, we are conditioned to refrain from expression. We can be so tight-lipped. Sometimes, the only thing you can get out of us is, "Yo what's up man?" What's up with that though? God created us to be expressive beings. There is no need to repress the cognitive power or creative intelligence, that is contained within you. We often place the caution tape around ourselves that reads, "do not cross" because of past hurt. It is to our advantage and the ultimate benefit of others, that we begin to open up ourselves. We must first open ourselves to God, to experience the magnanimity of His blessings. He has the power to heal and lift us higher.

VALUE YOU

You rarely hear that a man, should know his worth and value himself. It's a topic often reserved for women. However, our true value is not contained in our money or a list of women. Sexual conquests do not quantify or qualify us. It is not a trophy or badge of honor. Romans 12:1 implores us, "Present your bodies as a living sacrifice, holy, acceptable unto God which is your reasonable service." Your body is a temple and God only inhabits places of purity. No longer can we engage in illicit, illegal, and self-destructive behaviors that diminish our lives. We can't destroy each other's lives through violence and crime. No longer can we berate our sisters or call them anything but a queen and a child of God. We should not harass, abuse, or disrespect them. We must love, honor, and protect them. Now is the time to improve the   impoverished areas and facets of life. It begins with us interpersonally. It's time to recognize your true value within.

PASSION AND PURPOSE

God seeks to align and direct our passions as men. He desires to use passionate men, but those passions must first be directed toward God. As men, we are invigorated internally with intensity and desire. The very nature of sports, showcases men who possess these characteristics. As a result, it propels them to do exploits in arenas. Our passions can propel us to power, yet at the same time plummet us into a state of self-pity. Our passions are often triggered by sensations. The world operates from the basis of stimulating our senses. Your passion and competitive drive must be controlled. If not, you will impulsively make permanent decisions in temporary situations.

I Corinthians 7:32 declares, "He that is unmarried careth for the things that belong to the Lord, how he may please the Lord." As an unmarried man, your passion and purpose, must be aligned with the will of God for your life. Our actions should focus on growth and spiritual commitment, not solely self-fulfillment. When our desires our aligned with God in our singleness, it presents an opportunity for Him to bring us into a place of wholeness.

BLINDED BY BEAUTY

The Motown sound of the Temptations, provided the lyrics to the song, *Beauty Is Only Skin Deep*. It was a forewarning, of the temptations that life brings. Yes, she may very well possess a voluptuous physique or a fine frame. There's nothing wrong with admiring. It only becomes a problem when it transforms to lusting. However, albeit the grandeur of her pulchritude, you must remain alert and vigilant. Don't become so fixated on the outside, that you fail to discover who she is from within. You don't need a vixen. You need a virtuous woman. As men, we must also embody that virtue with our faithfulness and how we live too.

A real queen who possesses the qualities of a wife, will genuinely be interested in you. She will love you for you, not because of what you can do. She understands that you as a person are greater than your profession. She's not after what is in your pockets. Rather, she desires to help you fulfill your purpose. Beyond what is in your wallet, she wants to glean from your level of wisdom. She is a woman of wisdom. Not only is she your favor, but she will also give you wisdom.

Various scriptures refer to wisdom as a woman. Proverbs 8:1, 2 declares, "Does not wisdom call out? Does not understanding put forth her voice? She standeth in the top of high places." The wisdom of a woman will add greatness to your life. When you find a wife, not only do you receive favor but wisdom is a byproduct too. Her insight will lift you to higher heights.

Never allow your visual acuity to skew your integrity. Don't allow yourself to be blinded by beauty. It's only a skin deep mirage. It will attract you, but only the depth within her spirit and soul will keep you. What good is it for a woman to smell like an intoxicating fragrance, but her attitude is like

an odor? The right attitude will lift you to a greater altitude.

God desires to take us from where we are, to where

we can be. First, He has to teach us individually, to help us

get there collectively. If you stand on my shoulders and I

propel you over the wall of life, don't move on and leave me

where I am. Since I helped you, then reach back to help me.

We must reach back to mentor, inspire, and lift our brothers.

LOST AND FOUND

Our brothers are searching for true freedom. Your brother is

struggling to maintain his character. Another brother is faced

with the pressures of life and striving to make sound

decisions. We are all in this fight together. No one of us,

is greater than all of us. We need brothers with spiritual

discernment. They can probe into the hearts of the confused,

misused, and abused. We need brothers that will open their

arms to the lost and assist them. If you have yourself

together, then help somebody else. If you have overcome, then turn around and help somebody do the same.

We may not be related biologically, but we're joined together spiritually and in our community. In Galatians chapter 6, the Apostle Paul cautions us through the restoration of others, not to be haughty or high-minded. Arrogance and pride will make you believe that you have matriculated, to a higher echelon of nobility. You have to let the ego, go! We cannot be puffed up with pride.

Our confidence must be in something greater than ourselves. Despite how serene or stable life seems, don't become lackadaisical and place total security in yourself. Remain vigilant and sober minded. Stop comparing yourself to other people. Oftentimes, as men that is our greatest malady. We are so competitive toward one another, that we fail to collaborate and strengthen each other. Don't compare your progress to another individual's success. Nobody can beat you, being you. Stay in your lane and run your race, so you won't crash. II Corinthians 10:12 warns us against comparing ourselves with one another. You add unnecessary pressure to yourself, when you compete with someone else. Consequently, you take your eyes off your purpose and hinder your progress.

MAN OF HONOR

Where are the men of honor today? Do you consider yourself to be one? Don't let the media fool you. There are still good men like you, who are present in homes, schools, churches, and communities. Our world needs you more than ever before. Don't be a spectator. You must heed the clarion call, as an active participator in the cultivation of lives.

Our world is waiting on you to restore, resurrect, and revitalize the lives of men, women, and children. You were created to be a man of might and the model of God's magnitude. Take your rightful place as a man of valor. Be the role model that others look to for guidance. Be the man of strength and reconciliation, by dispensing the revelation of God's Word in action. You may have been broken, but God is mending your soul. You may have experienced hurt, but God can heal you. The value of restoration in your brother's life, is not only a benefit but a true necessity.

MY BROTHER'S KEEPER

It's necessary that we as brothers, come together on one accord. If we are divided against each other, then we cannot stand united with one another. Looking sharp on the outside means nothing, if you're dull on the inside. Proverbs 27:17 declares, "Iron sharpeneth iron; so a man sharpeneth the countenance of his friend." The world needs your sharpness, inner fortitude, and testimonies of the trials you have overcome. We must sharpen one another with ideas, encouragement, cooperation, and unity. As a result, our children and communities will sharpen and shape up. It's time to infuse strength and vitality into the life of your brother. You are your brother's keeper.

The death of every man diminishes who you are. Let's work to keep our brothers alive and prosperous. The blood of the slain in the streets is crying out. Are we receptive enough, to see the pain that so many are blind to? The blindness is not simply physical, it's mental and spiritual. Empower and share your testimony by giving insight. Our young brothers may not be your biological sons, but we can't shun them. We have to adopt and show love to them. We must extend our hands and hearts, in order to enhance our families, relationships, and communities.

WHOA MAN

A woman is the completion of God's creation. If you think about it, we as men are the rough draft. A woman is the final copy. Yes, she communicates differently and thinks differently, but she can complement us uniquely. Sometimes we don't understand a woman. However, her being different does not mean she's deficient. Even in Genesis chapter 2,

God did not create Adam and Eve together. Eve did not come on the scene until Adam had a purpose, place, presence, and power. Adam's purpose was to keep and maintain the Garden of Eden. So the man had an occupation. Adam's place of residence was in the Garden. He had presence. Not solely his own presence, but He had the presence of God. He communed and fellowshipped with God. How can you lead her, if God is not leading you? Adam also had power. God gave him dominion, over the beasts of the field and the fowl of the air.

The aforementioned qualities enabled Adam to have a purpose partner. As a man, if I don't have order in my life, then I shouldn't pursue a woman and make her my wife.

A woman was not created to operate in chaos. Notice, Eve was not even placed on the planet, until everything was in place. She was taken from the rib of Adam. Brother, you know you have the right rib, when you can breathe a lot easier. If she's compressing your calling and stressing you, instead of blessing you, then she's not the one for you. She will add to you as an asset, not subtract from your strength as a liability. In Genesis 2:23 Adam said, "Bone of my bones and flesh of my flesh. She shall be called Woman."

Upon Eve being created, Adam literally located and recognized himself in her. Bro, you must realize the importance of having the right woman. The right one will make you say, "Whoa man" and "Amen." The wrong one will cause you to say, "Oh man." Who God created, surprised Adam. The right woman will put you in such amazement and awe, that her standards will make you step up your game. She will upgrade your life and inspire you to aspire higher. The woman that God has prepared for you, will surprise you and bless you. The right woman will make you thank the Lord, for her existence and presence in your life. Her aura and essence will make you say, "Where have you been all of my life?"

ALONE BUT NOT ALONE

In Genesis 2:18, God said, "It is not good that the man should be alone; I will make him an help meet for him." If you've grown up in church like me, it's generally conveyed that God is all we need. However God said, "It's not good for man to be alone." Yet the prevailing question is, "How can I be alone, if God is there?" Consider and ponder that thought with me. If God is all I need and He is there, then how can I be alone?

God said, "It is not good for man to be alone." The emphasis doesn't necessarily mean that being alone is bad. The word "good" speaks to being beneficial, economical, or practical. It's not morally, physically, or financially bad to be by yourself. Yet the context of the text, speaks to the aspect that it's not conducive or desirable. It's not advantageous to the totality of happiness and well-being, to be by yourself.

At the core of human existence, no one truly desires to be by themselves. God created us to be social beings. Although you connect to an invisible God, you still need to connect to someone who you can see visibly.

The etymology of the word "alone" means to be solitary, separated, and isolated. It's interesting what the Creator does. God said, "It's not good for man to be alone," after He created Adam by himself. Imagine Adam walking through the Garden of Eden. He looks around and notices two horses, two dogs, two elephants, two giraffes, two birds, and two lions together. Where is his partner? As brilliant as Adam was, I'm sure it didn't take him long to figure out that he was the only one without someone.

God is above you and the animals are below you, but you need someone to be a suitable fit for you. Single and selective with standards is better than lowering them, for companionship with no compatibility. If you have somebody and they're not on your level, you're still alone!

BY YOUR SIDE

I often hear the phrase, "Behind every great man is a great woman." I know it sounds good, but the phraseology is utterly wrong. It's not behind but "Beside every great man is a great woman." I find it intriguing that God did not create the woman from the skull, so she could usurp your authority. God did not create the woman from the plantar bone of the foot, so you would step on her. Neither did He create the woman from the man's vertebral column, so he could be in front of her.

However, God created the woman from the man's rib, which is from the side of his anatomical structure. This is because a woman was created to be your helpmate and remain by your side. Brother, you don't have to be in front of her to lead her. You can still lead her, if she has more education and money than you. If you have a vision, you can lead her. You can walk hand in hand with her, right by your side. A real man doesn't want his woman behind him. He wants her beside him. Yes, even during tough times of tests and trials.

A woman with the qualities of a wife is successful, but she's also helpful. She is designed to support you and sees things from a different view. As you're looking at it, she can see around it and through it. Her helpful perspective is supportive.

However, as men sometimes the last thing we want is help. From finding the destination when driving, to picking up a heavy item, or even locating what we've lost. We say, "I got this. I'll figure it out. I don't need any help." We must not see receiving help as weakness. It's strength when your purpose partner, desires to assist you and you allow her to do that. When you let the ego, go then you can grow with who God has for you. Expect provision as a covenant companion, to lead and love your wife as a strong husband.

PRAY, PROVIDE, AND PROTECT

Are you tried, tested, and approved to be a husband? A man pursuing the life of a husband must be prepared to pray, protect, and provide for his wife. Your leadership ability must be equipped, by having a vision for provision.

The role of a husband is to be a provider and protector. It begins with leadership. He must provide for her needs, care for her well-being, and protect the family. A husband is the priest of his home. God's daughters are divinely designed with a purpose in mind. A man who desires a wife should be faithful, express love, protect, and provide for the well-being of her life.

We can clearly see that women are very capable and well-equipped to take care of themselves. Many would argue that they're smarter than us. They are more educated. They build businesses. They are self-sufficient and will even put their children's needs before their own. However, a woman who is in the care of her husband, should be provided for and protected. If not, then that man is not fit to lead her. Our physical strength should not be used to subdue, subjugate, or abuse her. Our strength should be managed with grace and gentleness. Neither the man nor woman was created to dominate one another, but to complement each other. They are purpose partners and covenant companions.

What are you willing to give up, for your wife or future wife? Are you willing to let go of pride, a false sense of masculinity, irresponsibility, ego, and impulsiveness? You can't expect peace from a woman, if all you bring her is stress and misery. You can't expect her to stay, if you give her every reason to leave and receive better. Realize that she is loyal to you because she has integrity and self-respect, not because she lacks options. Someone else will gladly treat her better, if you take her for granted. Too often, we don't realize how good a woman is to us, until she decides to leaves us. Don't let her ultimatum or decision to leave you, be the only reason you're awakened to her value. See it and secure your position in her life, to remain in it.

You can't expect a woman to submit to you, just because you see yourself as "the man." Submission goes beyond your muscles, money, or Mercedes. What vision do you have, that gives her a clear understanding of what to submit to? A woman will always honor and respect a man with a plan. She wants direction, leadership, protection, and the feeling that "my baby got this." It will make her receptive enough, to follow your lead as God leads you.

Prior to the fall of man in the Garden, Adam was following God and Eve was following Adam. However, sin reversed everything. Now the man was following the woman, but God doesn't follow anybody. Leadership and vision is a requirement for restoration. My brother, even as you're reading, God is removing the blinders from your eyes. You will see your destiny with clarity. The generational curses of neglect, brokenness, unspoken pain, and shame are being broken from your life. Despite the bad examples of how to treat a woman and what it means to be a man, you will become who God created you to be.

COVENANT COMPANIONSHIP

A husband must love his wife as Christ loved the church. A wife must also respect the leadership of her husband, as his helpmate. As spouses, you both should work in tandem to love, respect, and support one another. A covenant of companionship was first set in Genesis. Adam needed a companion and a suitable helpmate. However, one could not be found until God created Eve.

According to Genesis 2:24, "A man leaves his father and mother and is united to his wife, and they become one flesh." As a support system, covenant companion, and purpose partner, you must understand that your differences are not deficiencies. Your diversity is not adversity, but strength personified when united. Where one is weak, the other is strong. One should not diminish the other because of weaknesses. Love, encouragement, and strength should be supplied.

LEADER, LEAD HER

The same example that applies in Genesis, must apply for our generation. Before you run after her, make sure you run after God. Before you pursue a woman, pursue your purpose as a man. You won't even be able to keep her, if you don't know how to be a leader. Love her and lead her. You truly can't lead her, if you're not a leader. A lack of leadership and wholeness in your singleness, can create a marital mess. Allow God to give you a vision, to first be led by Him. Where God guides, He will provide. Real leadership is not controlling or domineering. It causes you to cooperate, by complementing each other's gifts and talents. Our character, commitment, and compassion is harnessed through strength not weakness. As men we lead best, when we love most.

HUSBAND = HOUSE BAND

The definition of the word "husband" is the result of combining the words, "house" and "band." A husband must be a house band, who enables via provision and protection. His job is to bind, secure, strengthen, encircle, and tie the household together for the purpose of unity. Society often relegates the job of keeping a house together to a woman. However, a husband must ensure that order is maintained in the house via the power of direction and vision. We should not be controlling but loving.

As a husband and house band, you must be a cultivator and communicator. Discover new ways to bring out the greatness in your wife. A husband manages and maintains the daily tasks at hand. He is a good steward who yields profits in his career, relationships, and home. He is not lacking, but focused on creating and producing.

Like any house band that comprises a group of

musicians, there must be an arranger or musical director. A husband must have keen eyes and ears to arrange, direct, manage, and assess. He should ensure that things work together to create a sound of harmony, rather than a cacophony. Undoubtedly, there are married men who are not husbands, because they fail to operate in leadership as the band of their house. In some cases, the wife has become "the husband" because she leads, manages, instructs, and keeps the daily operations of the house afloat. When there is a lack of order, there will always be chaos and disorder. A husband must ensure that his wife and children, are on beat and in sync with the rhythm of God's vision.

MARRIAGE-MINDED MAN

If you consider yourself to be a king and find a woman with the qualities of a queen, treat her accordingly. Know your identity and walk in a place of maturity. We must adopt a marriage-minded mentality. There is something to be said about a king who is preparing himself, to give a ring to his queen. The favor on our life increases when we marry a prepared wife, who has blessings attached to her life. Loving and valuing her, will strengthen her as a woman and empower us as men. God is releasing marriage-minded men who have a desire to love, provide, respect, and protect their woman.

I Corinthians 11:3 declares, "But I would have you know, that the head of every man is Christ; and the head of the woman is the man; and the head of Christ is God." A man should lead his spouse and house, as Christ leads him. We can't expect a woman to submit to us, if we are not fully submitted to God.

Colossians 3:19 affirms, "Husbands, love your wives and do not be harsh with them." What is your disposition and attitude? Are you kind and caring or mean and angry? How often are we just like Adam? Upon their sinful transgression in the Garden, he blamed Eve for what God told him to do. Still today, we blame women for what we know to do. Ephesians 5:25 declares, "Husbands, love your wives, just as Christ loved the church and gave himself up for her." What are you willing to give up, for your wife or your future wife? Are you willing to give up your ego, attitude, impulsiveness, or unfaithfulness? What is it that you're willing to sacrifice? She is a member of the body of Christ, but also a part of you, as you both have become one flesh. The intent of your love, should be conveyed in the extent of your sacrifice.

DEAR FUTURE WIFE

While she's preparing for you, she is also praying for you. Realize your future wife will love you, beyond what you do and see your true value. More than your profession, she's marrying a genuine person. As a future wife, be a present prayer warrior. Pray that your future husband walks in purpose, on the path to proposing to you. Pray that God molds him, into the man that He's called to be.

As she prays for you, pray for her too. In your time of meditation and devotion, pray that your future wife (as your rib) will help you breathe easier. Pray that she makes your vision come alive. Pray that her heart is open to trust you and be vulnerable with you. Pray that she will be a helpmate, to assist you and fulfill the purpose God gave you. Pray that she has wisdom and discernment, to see those who desire to prey on you. Pray that God gives you the integrity, to be a husband that loves, honors, provides, and protects her completely. She is praying that you will honor and love her, even when you don't completely understand her.

Just like you want her to be a praying wife. She needs you to be a praying husband. As you're praying and preparing for her, she is praying and preparing for you. God is preparing both of you, to unite as purpose partners. Brother, your prepared queen is rare and the answer to your prayers. She is the type of wife, that you need in your life!

PRAY TO GET HER, PRAY TOGETHER

If you prayed to get her, then also pray together. Don't prey on her, but pray with and for her. Too many men want a wifey and not a wife. They want the benefits without the commitments. Proverbs 18:22 declares, "He that findeth a wife" not a girlfriend. The right one is a woman of quality. She is worth committing to because of her value. The favor on her life will increase you.

More than what she can do for you, focus on what she can do with you. Can she communicate instead of argue? Can she pray with you? Can she support the vision God gave you? Can she be an asset as a spouse, supportive mother, and make a house a home? As you seek a wife, prepare by adding wisdom and wealth to your life. Don't waste your time or play with her. She is the right rib, that will make you breathe easier. She's a helpmate, who can ease the stress and bless you. She maintains the essence of a keen queen. God is aligning everything, so she can support you as a king. Lead her, pray, provide, and protect her. She will nurture, support, and strengthen you. As an asset, she will assist your vision for provision. A man who finds a good woman like her, finds favor. Don't sleep on her value. Stay woke! She's the kind of wife that will enhance your life.

Bro, I know you don't want a woman who has been with every man. Neither does she want a man, who has been with every woman. Sis, what a man wants from you, must also be what he adheres to. Relationships can't be double standards. The purity that we expect from you, must also be exhibited within us as men too. What we require from a woman, is what we should bring to the table. You really don't have anybody, by being with everybody. We must learn to value quality over quantity. When you know that you are somebody, you carry yourself differently. You recognize that your presence is a present and are cautious of who you allow into your space.

WHO'S CHOOSING WHO?

What happens when you're looking, but not finding? People often make snap judgments and ridiculous statements such as, "All of these women out here. You should be married by now." The statement is in error because they inaccurately conjecture, that quantity means compatibility and suitability. However, finding a quality purpose partner that's truly tailor-made for you or me is a rarity. Some people want you to hurry up and marry, just to join their misery. They failed to wait on God. Now they want to hurry you, to choose someone who isn't the best choice for you.

There is a school of thought called, "The paradox of choice." It derives from the notion that more is actually less. Sometimes when you have too many choices, you don't pick anything. As a result, you may end up choosing someone who chooses you. In many cases, that can be a bad choice for you. This is why allowing God to direct your passion and purpose, is so vital to your growth. It also keeps you in a place of wholeness not brokenness, so that you become a suitable purpose partner. It's easy to find quantity. The real value is in being a man of quality and attracting a woman who reflects the same. When there is no duality in your identity, God can give you clarity for proper decision making. God is preparing me. I'm developing my life, so that I can provide and be an asset to my future wife.

THE "S" ON HER CHEST

To the world she's Superwoman, but the "S" on her chest doesn't always mean she's strong. Sometimes she's sensitive, struggling, and needs to be supported. She's made sacrifices. How many will you make for her? She's had to be strong for so long, but she needs your shoulder to lean on. She even knows how to put on a smile when she's feeling down. Hold her hand, instead of your phone. Gaze at her smile, not your screen. Straighten her crown, lift her chin, and look her in the eyes. Remind her that she's beautiful, blessed, bright, brilliant, and bold.

Learning how to touch her without touching her, truly touches her. Many males desire to touch her sexually, but will you be the man to touch her soul spiritually? She's not like everybody. She's made uniquely. Take the time to embrace her queen quality with love and sensitivity. No, she may not be a supermodel, but she has the qualities of a role model. If you're solely focused on her physical assets on the outside, you will miss her intangible and spiritual value on the inside. Don't sacrifice someone of substance, to settle for something superficial. Don't trade what's permanent for something temporary. Start building, what you intend on sustaining in the future. A king and queen will always be secure in each other's hands, when they place their trust in God's hands. See it before you see it, so you can receive it. Your wife will be a blessing to your life. Prepare to love and lead her, as an honorable husband and leader.

SHE CAN UPGRADE YOU

Every king needs a queen to pray with him, for him, and encourage him. A queen will be good to you and for you. She wants the best for you, because she sees the best in you. She wants to bless you, not stress you. When you have a queen, you both make a powerful team. When the weight of the world is on you, she will minister a word of healing to you. A queen is the kind of wife, that adds value to her king's life. God will bless you to find your equal. She will know how to play her part and let you take the lead role. She won't fight against you. She will fight for you. She's a soldier of love and a freedom fighter of faith. You don't just need anyone, you need the right one. A queen can empower you to face anything, as you fulfill your dream. Don't reduce or downgrade her. To have her as your wife, is an upgrade to your life.

Date and pursue her, like you're still trying to get her, when you already have her. Pursue her like you did, when you were first in pursuit of her. The roses, dinner dates, love notes, and special gifts are great for holidays and birthdays. However, it means more to her, when it's "just because" on a regular day. The "I just called to say I love you" conversations will express your affection. She's worth the chase and one you can't replace. Don't get the woman that everyone wants and forget she's still the woman that someone wants. The key to keeping her, is to continually date and pursue her, when you already have her. Treat her like a queen because she's your queen.

CHAPTER 12

Without Further "I Do"

Marriage is not about finding someone that you can live with. It's about loving someone that you can't live without.

So the song goes, "If you liked it, then you should have put a ring on it." The *Single Ladies* anthem seems to be more than just a pop culture catch phrase, echoing mellifluously and melodiously from Beyoncé Knowles-Carter.

Now if you've seen the video, any man would be distracted by the calisthenics and gyrations. Yet there is a message of substance amidst the shaking. If I asked the single ladies across America to raise their hands, 51% would acknowledge their unmarried status.

There was a popular saying in the 1990s, "You go, girl!" which was used as a term of endearment and encouragement. These days the saying can arguably be rephrased, "You go girl and get married." Get married to who though? A recent Yale study, indicates that fewer women are walking down the aisle. Roughly 23 percent of White women and 42 percent of African-American women, have yet to be married.

SEEK AND YOU WILL FIND?

The wise saying in Proverbs 18:22 declares, "He that findeth a wife, findeth a good thing and obtaineth favor of the Lord." So, are men not looking or are they not finding? Looking and finding are two different things. You can be looking for something that you will never find. Especially, if it's a false pretense of the qualities in an individual.

According to Time Magazine's article, "Who Needs Marriage?" in 1960 nearly 70% of American adults were married. Now, only about half are married. In 1960,

two-thirds of 20-somethings were married. In recent years

just 26% were married.

TO MARRY OR NOT TO MARRY?

So, is marriage becoming obsolete? Well, according to the

Pew Research Center Survey, 4 in 10 believe so. It is no

secret that approximately 60% of marriages end in divorce.

The troubled state of our unions, indicate that marriage is

becoming less popular in America.

Why are 60% of marriages ending in divorce? For a

myriad of reasons, as we have heard on talk shows or seen in

our homes. Much is due to an inability to resolve conflicts,

infidelity, poor communication, finances, lack of identity,

and vision to name a few.

In chapter 4, I proposed did Tyler Perry get the

question correct in his film, *Why Did I Get Married?* All of

the aforementioned factors which lead to divorce, have now

made people ask, "Why would I get married?"

MARRED MARRIAGES

As 60% of marriages end in divorce, 40% of people believe there is no need for marriage. Our country is in a crisis and at a crossroads. The institution of marriage is under attack and in the crosshairs of this country. What has brought our nation to this point?

Just turn back the hands of time 50 years, to see how popular culture mirrored society. We have transitioned from the wholesome households of The Cleavers (*Leave It To Beaver*), *The Brady Bunch,* and *Family Matters* to now a false sense of reality TV age. Now you see TV shows like *Basketball Wives, Love & Hip Hop,* and *Keeping Up With The Kardashians* style of living, dating, and marriage.

Going back some 50 years, many women had a degree in domestic engineering. Now, it's the norm for women to specialize in fatherless home child rearing, all while earning a degree and building a business. Oftentimes, mothers are told "Happy Father's Day Mom" from children who grow up in fatherless homes.

The fight for the family is stronger than ever before. American culture shows the rapid transition in the familial landscape, as we have transitioned from *Family Ties* to *Cheaters* and *Divorce Court*. The Bible affirms in Mark 10:9, "What therefore God hath joined together, let not man put asunder." However, marriages are being put asunder. So many are eager to "jump the broom." Ironically, that same broom is used to sweep unresolved issues under the rug.

CARATS OR CHARACTER?

The woes of marriage are not excluded from our house, the White House, and even the church house. Can I get a witness? You know how it goes. They met at church and began dating. She dated thinking he was her Boaz. They got married and she discovered he was a bozo.

He thought she was the Biblical version of Ruth. He discovered she wasn't telling the truth. He was tall, dark, and a deacon, but he couldn't stop sneaking. She had curves like the letter "S," but the sister was really a snake. A friend of mine said to me, "Just because she has a Coke bottle body on the outside, doesn't mean the pop ain't flat on the inside."

Quite hilarious yet truthful. Indeed and in fact, we all have our perspectives, proclivities, and stories. Sadly, in a superficial society, we have become so focused on the size of the carat. Consequently, we have lost sight of substance and character.

How does your church address marital issues? Do you believe counseling and therapy can be a remedy? Who is preparing men and women to be husbands and wives? What can we do to prepare them for marriage? Something is wrong if we just continue to buy clothes that cover our issues, but refuse to deal with the naked truth about who we are.

It's wrong if we continue to see families torn apart, in our communities, but drive by as if nothing happened. Something is wrong if we just continue to build churches, collect offerings, and stand on the sidelines while marriages are marred and families fall apart. It's one thing to build buildings, but it's another thing to build people.

TUNNEL VISION

Our society has gone from *Married with Children* to *The Maury Show* headline, "He is not the father of your children." The false sense of reality TV with baby daddy and baby mama drama, glorifies pain which cripples our families and communities. The high drama increases ratings, but diminishes lifestyles. I'm beginning to see, why they call shows "TV programs." The minds of our youth are so malleable, that various shows actually "program" their minds. You have to literally watch what you watch. Oftentimes, it's more negative than positive. Many television programs have given Americans tunnel vision, to promote

negativity and consumerism.

I DO, I DON'T, OR I WON'T

How do you introduce the relevance of marriage, to an "I'm

doing me generation?" Cohabitation continues to increase.

Since 1960, there are now eight times more out of wedlock

births. Many are resorting to just live together, than to marry

and be happily ever after.

Is it still possible to say, "I do" in an iPhone, iPad,

Instagram, Facebook, and YouTube generation? We're living

in a world today, that spells the word "we" with two "I's."

I'm referring to the *Wii* video game system.

Even the names of our techno gadgets, are indicative

of a narcissistic ideology and society. We live in an age that

conveys, it's all about "I and you." Is there enough

selflessness within our hearts, to switch the focus to "us and

we?" How do you build a long-lasting relationship and

marriage, in an instant gratification society? People aren't waiting seven years to scratch their itch anymore. If you desire to be married, what is your motive? Is it love, money, loneliness, sense of obligation, sex, control, age, etc?

Some women flaunt their body, while many men parade their money. After the rendezvous is over she cries, "He only wanted me for my body." He says, "She only wanted my money." Well, if that's only what you showcase and promote, then that is all you will attract. You can't expect people not to have an appetite, if all you bring to the table is money and meat.

Where is our value? What are your values? If you're exchanging your self-worth and character in hopes of carats, then you will face the spectrum of disappointment. If you don't remedy the damaging relationships of the past, it will bring about a jaded perspective for the future. Bro, you shouldn't have to bribe her, to make her your bride. Sis, don't give a man an ultimatum or beg him to marry you. If you had to do all of that to get them, then you will have to do even more to keep them. It's not worth holding on to someone, who has no intentions of growing with you.

I'm beginning to realize, that marriage is not about finding someone that you can live with. It's about loving someone that you can't live without. It's God's design to prepare you, for who and what He has in mind. You're not wasting or losing time. He is preparing who you're marrying. Be encouraged and know that everything is aligning, for your purpose partner, support system, and covenant companion.

IT'S NOT A RACE, IT'S A PACE

Is the spectrum of engagement and marriage, only relegated to a woman being the envy of her girlfriends? Is it solely for the purpose of posting an engagement ring on a social site? Are people desiring to only marry for the wedding? Marriage is not a race, it's a pace. It's not a sprint, it's a marathon. Some people are ready for a wedding, but unprepared for a marriage. More than a celebration, it takes real commitment and dedication. The objective is not to just get married. It's to stay married. Saying "I do" is about more than a wedding day. It's what your actions say each day. If you don't have the right mentality, when tough times come, you will always find an exit strategy. More than a title, are you truthful? Beyond carats, what's your character?

The ugly relationship you went through, won't compare to the beautiful marriage that God has for you. The wrong one stressed you, but the right one will bless you. Despite all of the times that you were hurt, you tried to make it work. Don't give up on love, this time it will work. It's best to be with someone who is in shape spiritually, mentally, physically, interpersonally, and financially. They will encourage you, to keep a pace for the long run.

What is it to have a big wedding ring and bill, but in your marriage you're not fulfilled? There are some weeds that grow after the wedding is over. If the garden of marriage is not pruned, then it won't last. Marriage is a merger. It's best to make sure, that your life intersects with the right individual, before you walk down the aisle. Remain prayerful and hopeful. God will bless you with the right person and your marriage will be beautiful.

WHY DO FOOLS FALL IN LOVE?

Personally, I don't want to fall in love. I don't want to fall into anything. Too many times, we fall for people who aren't capable of catching us. I prefer to grow in love with the right woman. I desire to stand in love with my future wife and purpose partner. When things go left, if you have the right teammate, your relationship and marriage will survive the storm. Everything will turn out right with someone who will continue to fight. You can't lose with a husband, who is a house band and a wife that will offset strife.

MARRIAGE IS A MERGER

God is answering the prayers you've been praying. Prepare your mind and heart, to receive the desires of your heart. The right man is coming, to make you his wife and add value to your life. Don't take the pain of your past into a new year. God is doing a new thing this year. New love. New divine connections. This time when you cry, it will be tears of joy. You won't be surprised by disappointment, but through enjoyment and fulfillment. Who God has for you, will only have eyes for you. It's about more than what they drive, but what drives them. More than their money, body, or status as a celebrity. It's their integrity to honor, provide, protect, and love you securely. Stop replaying a nightmare. God is preparing and pairing you with the spouse of your dreams.

HEART TO LOVE

Pray and prepare presently, for the spouse you're expecting eventually! As God is preparing you for them, He's preparing them for you. God will bring your spouse, when there is order in your house. Sometimes God won't give us what we want, because we're still connected to who we don't need. Don't expect Him to bless, disorder and mess. Keep working to become the best and receive His best. Just because they have a heart, doesn't mean they have a heart. A good heart like yours, deserves a good heart too. Their actions will show you, better than their words can tell you. Realize everyone doesn't have your best interest at heart. Pray for discernment, so you don't ignore the red flags and signs that you should recognize.

Real eyes, realize, real truth or lies. People can be candy to your eyes, but bad for your heart. Their actions are the ingredients, that will either revive or reduce you. Eyes can trick you and your heart can deceive you. Seek God for direction and discernment, so He can reveal what's real. Recognize the signs, to see if they're any good for you, before they become your bae, boo, or make you say "I do."

Don't stop being good, because somebody treated you bad. Maintain your good heart. It will attract real love that gives you a brand new start. Someone who really loves God, can really love you. Prepare for the right one, who has a heart for God and a heart to love you.

ONE DAY

You will be a blessing to your future spouse. Your "one day" can happen any day. Prepare to receive the love that you hope for, plus much more! The love you keep giving is coming. Get ready to receive your blessing. The right kind of love, will make up for all of the wrong ones, who took from you and withdrew. The one for you, is coming to deposit real love and value within you. Don't give up on love, you deserve it. Your heart is in the right place to receive it. God knows your heart and He's going to give you a brand new start. For all of the times you've questioned, get ready to see the real answer. The right one will appreciate and reciprocate, the love that you extend their way. Get ready to receive, all of the love you've given away. Pray and prepare now. It can happen any day!

IF YOU LOVE ME, PRAY FOR ME

Dear future wife, I know you will add value to my life. As you're preparing for me, please pray for me. Love me beyond what I do and see me for who I am. More than my profession, you're marrying a genuine person. Pray that I walk in my purpose, on the path to proposing to you. Pray that God molds me into the man, that He's called me to be as a faithful husband to you. Pray that as my rib, you help me breathe easier. Pray that my heart, is open to trust you and be vulnerable with you. Pray that as my wife, your wisdom improves my life. Pray that as my queen, you assist me to complete the vision and attain provision. Pray for discernment, to see those who desire to prey on me. Pray that God gives me the ingenuity to lead with integrity. Pray that He orders my steps to love, provide, and protect you completely. Pray that I continue to honor and love you, even when I don't always understand you. As you're praying for me, God is preparing me. We will walk together in unity. I will pray for you, as you pray for me. You're a queen that's rare and the answer to my prayers. The type of wife, who I need in my life.

PRESENTLY PREPARE

We must think critically and evaluate ourselves, before we are betrothed to someone. If you partner with the wrong person, the ramifications can be taxing. Marriage is not some type of taste test or product, with a money back guarantee. It's about more than tying the knot, jumping a broom, or going viral after you say your vows.

Marriage is indeed a life-long investment, being akin to business. The symbolic consummation of marriage is a merger. If you don't have the right partner and make the wrong investments, your marriage will go bankrupt.

In the marriage liturgy, "Till death do us part" does not mean until things fall apart. We must be sincere, sure, and committed to be true, before we ever say the words, "I do." God is preparing you, for what He's preparing for you! More than a wedding, God is aligning you at the right timing for the right marriage. Presently prepare for the future that you and your spouse will share. God is connecting you, with who He has for you in a special way. You're being prepared now, to be someone's wife for life. You're being prepared to be a husband, as the head of your home.

Just because it didn't work last time, doesn't mean it won't work this time. Don't look back, focus forward on something greater. It's coming! God will align you with the right one to renew you, so you can love again. Don't fight it or doubt it. God will do it! See it before you see it, so you can receive it! God is giving you His best. Realize that you are the right purpose partner, as a future husband and head of your household. You're the kind of wife, who will be a covenant companion and addition to his life.

Release the past and rejoice over your future. Remain committed to being *Wisely Inspired Faithfully Empowered.* God has a blessing for you that's unique and rare. Get ready to say "I do!" The right one will walk further into the future, with you for life, as husband and *WIFE!*

SUCCESS IN SINGLENESS

As a bonus, here are *10 tips to walk in wholeness, wellness, and success in your singleness!*

1. Develop a Strong Relationship with God.

The greatest connection that you should ever have, is a relationship with God. He is the ultimate purpose partner. When you have a spiritual foundation, you learn how to love yourself and others in a greater way. The relationship or marriage will never work, if your relationship with God isn't developed first and foremost. People are not your source. God is your source. He wants to do a new thing in you, but you have to trust and follow His direction to guide you. It is for your protection. God will give you insight through His Word, but you have to communicate with Him. If you partner with God, the blessings and benefits will far exceed anything that you can ever imagine.

2. Love Yourself.

Too many times we focus solely on our weaknesses. We become so self-critical, that we ignore the strengths that we possess. You can't expect anybody to love and appreciate who you are, if you don't love and appreciate yourself. Eventually, you will attract who and what you are, by the way you view and treat yourself. Know who you are and whose you are. When you don't know who you are, you leave it to people to define you. Love yourself, embrace your uniqueness, and know your worth!

3. Better Crew, Better You.

Make sure that the people in your life, are adding to your life. If not, then subtract them from your life. On your journey to destiny, you need assets not liabilities. Distance yourself from people who drain you of your time, energy, and patience. There are some people in your life, that you must bless and release. Sometimes you just have to love people from a distance. A better you, begins by surrounding yourself with a better crew. Why surround yourself with people, who only intend to bring drama and distort your dream? They will keep you in a place of negativity. Who you're connected to, determines what you're directed to. Disconnect yourself from negative people. Stay connected to those who challenge you, to be a better you.

4. Invest in Yourself.

Giving and investing, always creates room for more. It takes character to remain selfless, in a society of selfishness and self-aggrandizement. What you can give, is more powerful than what you can receive. How many clothes and shoes can you wear at one time? How many cars can you drive at once? We have become so inundated by what we can consume, that we don't take the time to invest and produce. Make an investment in yourself and in the lives of others. What you can give may not be monetary, but it can be your time which is far greater than money. Look within your

relationships and within your community. You will see that

every problem has a solution, which you can provide. There

is always a blessing that comes by blessing other people.

You can give without loving, but you can't love without

giving. Recognize that you are a blessing and be a blessing.

5. Focus on Your Focus.

Whether you're in the winner's circle or not, depends on the

people in your circle. You are who you hang around. You

will either be a chicken or an eagle, a chump or a champion,

a worrier or a warrior. Which will you choose? You can't be

a whiner and a winner at the same time. You can't expect

God to do something new, if you only focus on what's

behind you. Forget those things which are behind and press

toward the mark for the prize (Philippians 3:13, 14). I know

you went through a painful process, but it prepared you for a

greater promise and purpose. Your next move will be your

best move. This is your season of greater success. Despite the pain, trust God's plan. For all of the stress you went through, God is getting ready to blow your mind. He will make your enemies bless you. Keep the faith and focus on your focus. Get excited about what's coming next. It's about to happen now! Too often we focus on what everyone else is doing. As a result, we fail to do what we're supposed to do. Focus on Him, not them. Don't compete or compare. Just remain focused and prepare. Make a decision to press your way, toward the path of purpose and destiny each day. You can't win with a losers mentality. It's time to focus with urgency!

6. Pursue Your Purpose.

You will always put your purpose on pause, if you only live for applause. Stop seeking validation from people, who don't even know themselves. Focus on the purpose that God gave you, not who dislikes you. Don't get depressed by trying to impress people. Seek to please God instead. You don't need to seek anyone's permission, to walk in your purpose. You don't have to wait to be great. Make up your mind to mute the opinions around you, so you can hear the true voice within you. If you please God in the process, He will position you to pursue your purpose. When you recognize the God-given treasure within, you will see the enormous value that permeates your life. Love, respect, and value yourself through every negative circumstance and painful experience. There's a treasure in you! The tragedy is to be gifted and not open the package. You are packaged with purpose, promise, power, possibility, and potential. You are a red box and gold bow. A gift to the world. You must take personal inventory of your life. The best way to be found is by working your gifts, looking your best, and walking in your purpose.

7. Value You.

Invest in your value and become wealthy from the inside out. You can never go bankrupt, when you invest in yourself. See your true wealth and wisdom from within. To have a beautiful exterior with nothing in your mind, is like having a *Louis Vuitton* or *Gucci* bag with no money inside. Your value and worth, doesn't begin from the outside-in. It starts from the inside-out. Your value isn't tied, to what people think about you. It's in how you think about yourself. Get around people who enhance your value. Avoid the ones who diminish it. The more you value yourself, the more people will value you!

8. Let Go of the Past.

You won't live your best life, until you let go of anger, bitterness, and strife. You can't change the past, so why are you presently living in it? You have to let it go, in order to grow. Don't beat yourself up, over something you can't change. Stop reliving the memories of the past, that keep you living in the past. Don't run back to the same people, that God removed out of your life. Holding on to the past is a hazard and hindrance, to your hope and happiness. Life is about learning from your mistakes, not repeating the same missteps and living in the past. Don't take your past, into your present and future. You can't be free for your future, if you're still a slave to your past. Your past will confine you, but only your future will free you. It's over! Get up and move forward. Release the past, so you can step into your future.

9. Forgive to Live.

What are you holding on to, that's stifling your growth? Yes, there are certain pains that we have experienced. However, we must forge ahead in spite of the hurt. You even have to forgive those, who never gave you an apology. You will never become better, by being bitter. Forgiveness is freedom.

In order to truly live, you have to forgive. The hurt will transform into healing, when you put it in God's hands. Indeed, we have been victims, but we have also been perpetrators too. If God forgave you, then forgive yourself and others. Carrying the baggage of bitterness and resentment, will keep you limping with brokenness. It's time to leap to another level. Seek to forgive and seek to be forgiven. Your bountiful living, is connected to the power of forgiving.

10. Keep Going, Keep Growing.

In order to grow and get better, you have to continually put in the work to do it. Don't get lazy when it comes to laboring and building, to live your best life. There is no growth, without change and self-reflection. The power of self-development, is the key that unlocks the door to your destiny and opportunities. We live in a world of distractions. It's important to take the time to read, meditate, analyze your goals, and simply think. Growth brings with it growing pains because change is uncomfortable. Sometimes it hurts, to break away from bad habits and choices that aren't good for you. In the long run, what you do will either add to or subtract from you. It's either the pain of discipline or the pain of consequence. Ultimately, it's your decision. Take the necessary steps in your singleness, to live a life of wholeness and wellness, as you walk in greater success!

ACKNOWLEDGMENTS

Unbeknownst to me, was the fact that I was writing a trilogy. The completion of this project *Wife,* is the final series to prior books, *Dear Queen* and *Woman.* The culmination of the aforementioned, has brought an awakening and relief in its completion. My ninth book was literally a reflective mirror. Every chapter challenged me. The pages reinvigorated my perspective, on marriage much clearer. Undoubtedly, writing *Wife* as a single man was a rather bold move on my end. Very rarely, do we prepare men for marriage like we have done for women. I trust this is a blueprint.

Thank you to my Norbrook Publishing family, for their incredible work to unveil this project to the world. To my Mama Dr. Janice Connor, my brother Elijah, Don Smith, and Hawk. My gratitude extends to every contributor and supporter. Your encouragement is why I transparently share my journey. I strive to be a blessing to you, as you have been to me. Much love and thank you for reading *WIFE.* I pray it was a blessing to your life!

ABOUT THE AUTHOR

Dr. Eddie Connor is a bestselling author, college professor, international speaker, actor, and radio/TV correspondent. He is a survivor of stage four cancer and empowers people to overcome obstacles. Dr. Connor is the cousin of one of the world's most influential entertainers and musicians, the late legendary Prince.

As an author of nine bestselling books, Dr. Connor has been featured on BET, CBS, FOX, NBC, PBS, The Steve Harvey TV Show, The Tom Joyner Show, and The Word Network. He has been a guest on *The Potter's Touch* and as an empowerment speaker at Bishop T.D. Jakes' *MegaFest*. He was featured in the acclaimed BET documentary, *It Takes a Village to Raise Detroit*. He also stars in the movie, *Lady Luck...Too*.

Dr. Connor is the founder of the mentoring and reading program, *Boys 2 Books*, which empowers young males via literacy, leadership, and life skills enrichment. The program also became the impetus for President Barack Obama's, *My Brother's Keeper* initiative.

Dr. Connor is a recipient of *The President Barack Obama Volunteer Service Award* and *The President Barack Obama Lifetime Achievement Award* from The White House. He is recognized as one of the *Top 35 Millennial Influencers in America*, listed in the *Top 100 Leaders in Who's Who in Black Detroit*, and named to *Michigan Chronicle's Top 40 under 40*.

As a sought after communicator and motivator, he speaks extensively at churches, colleges, and conferences. Dr. Connor grew up in Kingston, Jamaica and lives in Detroit, Michigan. **Visit www.EddieConnor.com**

CONNECT WITH DR. EDDIE CONNOR

To request Dr. Eddie Connor for speaking engagements, media interviews, or for bulk book purchases, please email: **info@EddieConnor.com**

WEBSITE:
www.EddieConnor.com

SOCIAL MEDIA:
Facebook.com/EddieConnorJr
Instagram: @EddieConnorJr
Twitter: @EddieConnorJr
YouTube.com/EddieConnor
#WifeTheBook

Made in the
USA
Middletown, DE